QUALITY AUDITS FOR IMPROVED PERFORMANCE

Third Edition

Also available from ASQ Quality Press:

The Internal Auditing Pocket Guide
J. P. Russell

Quality Audit Handbook, Second Edition
ASQ Quality Audit Division

The ISO 9001:2000 Auditor's Companion
Kent A. Keeney

The ISO 9000 Auditor's Companion and The Audit Kit—Complete Set (2000)
Kent A. Keeney

Quality Audits for ISO 9001:2000: Making Compliance Value-Added
Timothy O'Hanlon

Fundamentals of Quality Auditing
B. Scott Parsowith

After the Quality Audit: Closing the Loop on the Audit Process,
Second Edition
J. P. Russell and Terry Regel

Internal Quality Auditing
Denis Pronovost

Puzzling Auditing Puzzles
Janice Russell and J. P. Russell

How to Plan an Audit
ASQ Quality Audit Technical Committee and Charles B. Robinson
(Editor)

Management Audits: The Assessment of Quality Management Systems,
Third Edition
Allan J. Sayle

To request a complimentary catalog of ASQ Quality Press publications, call (800) 248-1946, or visit our Web site at http://qualitypress.asq.org.

QUALITY AUDITS FOR IMPROVED PERFORMANCE

Third Edition

Dennis R. Arter

ASQ Quality Press
Milwaukee, Wisconsin

Quality Audits for Improved Performance, Third Edition
Dennis R. Arter

Library of Congress Cataloging-in-Publication Data

Arter, Dennis R., 1947–
   Quality audits for improved performance / Dennis R. Arter.—3rd ed.
      p.   cm.
   Includes bibliographical references and index.
   ISBN 0-87389-570-3 (Soft Cover, Perfect Bind : alk. paper)
   1. Quality control—Auditing.   I. Title.
TS156 .A76 2003
658.5'62—dc21

2002152028

10   9   8   7   6   5   4   3

ISBN 0-87389-570-3

Publisher: William A. Tony
Acquisitions Editor: Annemieke Koudstaal
Project Editor: Paul O'Mara
Production Administrator: Jennifer Gaertner
Special Marketing Representative: Robin Barry

ASQ Mission: The American Society for Quality advances individual, organizational and community excellence worldwide through learning, quality improvement and knowledge exchange.

Attention: Bookstores, Wholesalers, Schools and Corporations: ASQ Quality Press books, videotapes, audiotapes, and software are available at quantity discounts with bulk purchases for business, educational, or instructional use. For information, please contact ASQ Quality Press at 800-248-1946, or write to ASQ Quality Press, P.O. Box 3005, Milwaukee, WI 53201-3005.

To place orders or to request a free copy of the ASQ Quality Press Publications Catalog, including ASQ membership information, call 800-248-1946. Visit our web site at www.asq.org or http://qualitypress.asq.org.

Printed in the United States of America

∞ Printed on acid-free paper

American Society for Quality

Quality Press
600 N. Plankinton Avenue
Milwaukee, Wisconsin 53203
Call toll free 800-248-1946
Fax 414-272-1734
www.asq.org
http://qualitypress.asq.org
http://standardsgroup.asq.org
E-mail: authors@asq.org

Contents

Preface ix
  Acknowledgements ix
  Things both old and new x

Chapter 1   **Overview** 1
  Brief history of auditing 1
  What is an audit? 4
  General model of auditing 4
  Who's auditing whom? 5
  The compliance audit 6
  Shortcomings of the compliance audit 8
  Performance audits 9
  Performance audit applications 10
  Product audits 11
  Process audits 12
  System audits 15
  Six kinds of audits 17
  Audit defined 18
  Management principles 18
  Fundamental rules for auditing 19
  May auditors say good things? 20
  A different philosophy 20

Chapter 2   **Audit Program Manager** .23
  Accountability 23
  Audit schedule 23
  Resources for the audit program 24
  The client 27

Chapter 3   **Preparation** 29
  Phases of the audit 29
  Steps in the preparation phase 30
  Purpose 30

Scope 32
The audit team 33
Second rule of auditing 40
Authority 40
Requirements 41
Understand the process 46
Audit plan 48
Evaluate documents 52
Work papers 54
Summary 64

Chapter 4   **Performance** 67
Opening meeting 67
Gather the facts 70
Tracing 71
Interviews 72
Interview technique 73
Perceptions 78
Team meetings 79
Daily briefings 80
Onward 81

Chapter 5   **Reporting** 83
The report is your product 83
Report characteristics 83
Desire to trust 84
Inferences 84
Judgments 85
Pain and pleasure 85
Findings 86
Preparing the finding sheets 86
Recommendations 91
Presenting your information 92
Six or less 93
Overall conclusions 94
Exit meeting 94
Formal report 97
Report distribution 101
Distribution of the report 105
Wrap-up 106

Chapter 6 **Follow-up and Closure** 109
Closure phase 109
Remedial action 109
Corrective action 111
Corrective action response 113
Adequacy of the response 113
Records 114
A recap 116

Chapter 7 **Summary** 117

Appendix A **Example Procedure** 119
Purpose and scope 119
Definitions 119
Personnel qualification 120
Scheduling 120
Audit planning 121
Performance 122
Audit report 123
Follow-up 124
Records 124
Forms 125

Appendix B **Glossary of Terms** 127

Index 133

Preface

You are about to be introduced to some old and new approaches to the application of audits. Intense global competition and remarkable changes in technologies require us to challenge past practices. Old adversarial methods of seek, point, and blame will no longer work. Using some of the basic financial audit principles, we can examine the usefulness and implementation of all controls as they apply to internal and external operations. Audits, along with other forms of evaluation, can help us to determine if our own controls and our supplier controls work effectively.

Since this text was first published in 1989, some changes in auditing have taken place. The ISO 9001 standard, and conformity assessment to that document, caused interest in auditing to explode. With this intense interest in auditing, new ideas and techniques came along. The published literature has doubled in size and tripled in content. Auditing is now used around the world. Business and government are using the audit to improve the functioning of the enterprise. I have been fortunate to participate in this changing environment. Along the way, I discovered some underlying truths. Those truths are now quite clear to me. I hope they become clear to you.

ACKNOWLEDGEMENTS

Some major forces have influenced me in the past 30 years. As an officer in the U.S. Navy nuclear submarine force, I first learned about management and leadership principles. Upon leaving the Navy, I discovered the basic quality concepts while employed by a nuclear power utility. I also developed my basic audit skills. Although I had some help from the existing consensus standards, it was mainly a trial-and-error process. I made several mistakes, but I learned from them. I started training others in audit methods through the use of a package course developed in 1978 by Mr. Frank X. Brown for the U.S. Department of Energy. Seeing a need for auditing outside of the nuclear industry, I struck out on my own as a consultant in the fall of 1984. Since then, I continue to learn from each company I visit and each class I teach.

The American Society for Quality (ASQ) helped me more than I could have imagined. Networking with the Quality Audit Division and other groups in ASQ exposed me to different methods and uses for my chosen profession. Conference presentations force me to keep thinking. The Institute of Internal Auditors (IIA) and, of course, Larry Sawyer, helped me to put quality auditing in perspective with financial and operational auditing.

THINGS BOTH OLD AND NEW

Auditing, in its many forms, is a cost-effective means of improving the enterprise. The methods described in this book are both old and new. They may be difficult to accept and even more difficult to implement. They do, however, work. This book will cause you to think. Enjoy!

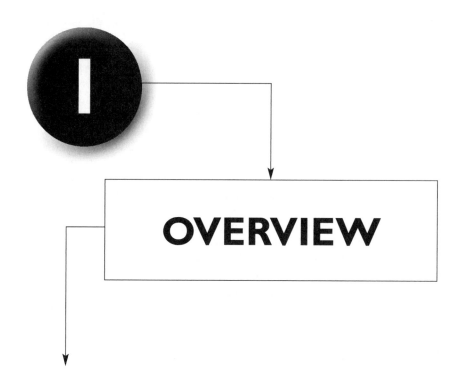

OVERVIEW

BRIEF HISTORY OF AUDITING

The word *audit* originally comes from the practice of recording the cargo on a ship by listening as the crew called out the items and quantities. The word comes from *aural* (to hear). The auditor represented the king and was there to provide assurance that all taxes on that cargo would be properly recorded.[1] From the very beginning, auditors were associated with controls and compliance. It is interesting to note that the original meaning of *audit* continues in a classroom setting. When you *audit* a class, you do not participate or receive credit on your transcript. You only listen.

Auditing, as practiced today, has its roots in financial applications. As Western civilization moved from the Middle Ages and into the Renaissance period, money lending became important for trade and kingdoms. There was a need for outside and unbiased assurance that both borrowers and lenders were telling the truth. Even today, the majority of auditors work in the financial services industries, such as banking, taxes, insurance, and accounting. Financial auditors are expected to examine the accounts and records to see that they are truthful. They match recorded information against accounting requirements to arrive at their findings of fact. Because the auditors are seen as unbiased, their reports are accepted by the stakeholders as truthful. Society will always have a need for financial auditors.

After World War II, the military was faced with tremendous new and powerful technologies with the potential to cause great harm. Tanks, bombs, and airplanes were much more complicated and quite risky. Nuclear energy, first used as a weapon of destruction, was being developed for civilian power generation. The 1950s were exciting times but also scary. In their search for tools to combat these new risks, the admirals and generals adapted the auditing methods of the accountants. One of the first quality management standards, MIL-Q-9858 (circa 1954), contained a brief paragraph on auditing. At the time, people really didn't know how to do it, but they knew it needed to be done. Like many other new things, we imposed the requirements on the suppliers but not ourselves. Perhaps our suppliers could figure it out.

Military and nuclear auditors working for the contractors started auditing their own programs. They began to audit the subcontractor's work. The government started auditing the contractors. They all made it up. Sometimes, it worked. Often, it didn't work. A decade later, by 1968, we had the beginnings of an auditing standard in the ASQC C1 document for supplier quality systems. It said, "Quality programs will be audited by the buyer for conformance to the intent of this specification. Disapproval of the program or major portions thereof may be cause for withholding acceptance of product."[2]

Meanwhile, the financial folks began to look outside of accounts payable and accounts receivable. The Institute of Internal Auditors (IIA) published their rules for operational auditing in 1978.[3] These continue to be updated and extensively used. Operational audits were developed to examine the controls and risks of the organization. They probed and questioned to find weaknesses that could lead to loss and fraud. The enterprise was becoming more complex and that complexity allowed bad things to occur. The operational auditor became an important line of defense for the smart enterprise. These auditors usually report to a committee on the corporate Board of Directors. They are often called *corporate auditors*.

Even the government people outside of military and nuclear areas began to examine the value of auditing their nonfinancial operations. Throughout the late 1970s and early 1980s, increased pressure demanded accountability for government operations and spending programs. The U.S. General Accounting Office, the investigative arm of Congress, first released their Government Auditing Standards in 1981. Because of the color of the cover, this was called the "Yellow Book." It continues to be an excellent source of information for all auditors.[4]

In response to the new global competition in the 1980s, manufacturers needed to change their ways of conducting business. They needed to do a better job of defining customer requirements. They needed to better control their manufacturing processes. They needed to gather data and make decisions from those data. They needed auditors. The U.S. standard on quality systems, Z-1.15 (1979), contains a pretty good description of those early internal and supplier audit quality programs.[5] The Canadians published their CAN3-Q395 document in 1981, based largely on the work done by the British and the IIA.[6] Even today, many of our auditing words can be traced to that Canadian standard. After much difficulty, the ASQ Quality Audit Division moved their version of the Canadian Q395 through the committees and it was published as Q1 in 1986.[7]

Auditing for software took a strange turn in the mid-1980s. In 1988, the Institute of Electrical and Electronic Engineers (IEEE) released standard 1028 called *Software Reviews and Audits.* The intent of these audits was to give project managers an indication of the thoroughness and completeness of an activity before it progressed to the next step. The audits were checks to see that all the paperwork was completed. These audits were not very valuable.

Interest in quality auditing for business applications really took off in the second half of the 1980s. The Cold War was ending. Communication technologies were developing into an Internet. World trade agreements were signed. All of this led to the first comprehensive international standard on quality management—ISO 9001 (1987).[8] The European Community, Canada, and Australia were the first to apply conformity assessment, formerly used for product certification, to the new standard. Of course, the registrars needed a standard for these third-party assessments. As they have done many times before, the British took a draft committee document and published it as BS7229 in 1989.[9] The approved international document came out two years later in three parts. ISO 10011-1 was published in December of 1990. Parts 2 and 3 came out in May of 1991. The United States took the three separate international documents and published them as one in 1994. It was called Q10011.[10] The 1981 Canadian Q395 was the foundation for all these national and international documents.

After the success of conformity assessment to quality management systems (ISO 9001), the environmental folks started doing the same thing with ISO 14001. Outside auditors were now conducting two sets of audits, at twice the price, and often looking at the same things. This wasn't very cost effective. Pressure was building for a common set of rules for both quality and environmental management system auditing.

Informal work on an integrated ISO 19011 auditing standard began in the mid-1990s and officially started in 1998. The group took on a huge task. Not only were they trying to build a common approach for quality and environmental auditors, but they were also trying to develop a common set of rules for internal, external, and even conformity assessment applications. Progress was painfully slow. The joint standard was finally issued in 2002.[11] It is still quite focused on conformity assessment applications, but progress is being made on codifying the profession.

WHAT IS AN AUDIT?

Although many people use the term audit, it is not always applied in a consistent manner. This is because people use words based on their previous experiences or what they have read. An audit means one of two things:

- State of completeness, or
- Performance of an activity to rules

An audit may be performed to see if everything is present and correct. To *audit* the records means to see if all the required records exist. It also means that those records have been checked for correctness. When used in this way, an audit is another word for 100 percent inspection.

The other meaning of *audit* involves the way things are performed. We examine an activity to see if it was done in accordance to the rules. The resulting analysis will tell stakeholders if the activity was conducted in accordance with planned arrangements and if those arrangements were successful in achieving the desired result. I believe this is closer to the historical use of the term.

GENERAL MODEL OF AUDITING

Many diverse organizations are using the process of having outsiders provide assurances to interested parties. We have quality auditors, financial auditors, environmental auditors, safety auditors, management auditors, operational auditors, tax auditors, and many more. All of these auditing schemes possess some common characteristics.

We must first have requirements for the item, activity, or organization. This is called the *basis* of the audit. We must also have facts relating to the implementation of those requirements. These are called *evidence*. When you compare the facts to the requirements, you get an *observation*, which can be either good or bad. So far, this is very much like an inspection. Auditors push on. They analyze these observations for patterns, which are called *findings*. Often, auditors are also requested to take all the observations, findings, sights, and smells, and draw *conclusions*. Their product, the *report*, is presented to interested parties for use. This can be seen in Figure 1.1, the general model for auditing. The remainder of this book will attempt to show you how to use the general model.

WHO'S AUDITING WHOM?

The audit can be accomplished by three different sets of auditors and auditees: first party, second party, and third party.

First-Party Audits

The first-party audit is also known as an *internal audit* or *self audit*. It is performed within your own company. This can be a central office group auditing one of the plants, auditing within a division, local audits within the plant, or any number of similar combinations. There are no external customer-supplier audit relationships here, just internal customers and suppliers.

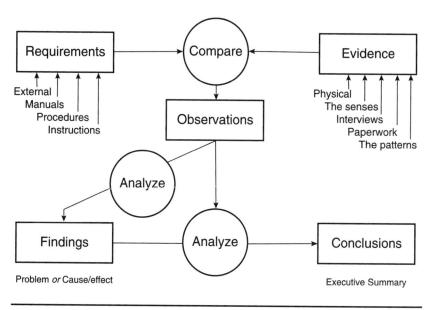

Figure 1.1 General model for auditing.

Second-Party Audits

A customer performs a second-party audit on a supplier. A contract is in place and goods are being, or will be, delivered. If you are in the process of approving a potential supplier through the application of these auditing techniques, you are performing a supplier survey. A survey is performed before the contract is signed; an audit is performed after the contract is signed. Second-party audits are also called *external audits*, if you are the one doing the auditing. If your customer is auditing you, it is still a second-party audit, but, since you are now on the receiving end, this is an *extrinsic* (not external) audit.

Third-Party Audits

Regulators or registrars perform third-party audits. Government inspectors may examine your operations to see if regulations are being obeyed. Within the United States, this is quite common in regulated industries, such as nuclear power stations and medical device manufacturers. Through these regulatory audits, the consumer public receives assurance that the laws are being obeyed and products are safe. Registration audits are performed as a condition of joining or being approved. Hospitals and universities are accredited by nongovernmental agencies to certain industry standards. Trade organizations may wish to promote the safety and quality of their industry products or services through an audit program and seal of approval. Other countries often use the term *certification* rather than *registration*. Businesses around the world are registering their facilities to the ISO 9001 standard in order to gain marketing advantage. Done properly, this registration promotes better business practices and greater efficiencies.

THE COMPLIANCE AUDIT

Audits can be divided into two categories by purpose: compliance and performance. A *compliance audit* looks for conformance to a set of rules. The rules may not be questioned; they are set. Examples of compliance audits include the following:

- **Tax audits.** Revenue agents at the local, state, and national level perform these audits. The agents check to see that taxes are reported and paid in accordance with the tax codes.
- **Financial audits.** These are the traditional audits of accounting controls, such as accounts payable, accounts receivable, and payroll. They are performed internally, within a company, or externally,

on another company. They give assurances to management and stockholders that the balance sheets and income statements are accurate. They are also designed to prevent (or minimize) waste, fraud, and abuse.

- **Regulatory audits.** The government regulates certain activities of society. Among these are the production of energy, the stewardship of the environment, the production of food, the protection of workers, and the use of medical devices. The health and safety of consumers are of prime importance in these regulated areas. Laws are passed and regulations are promulgated. Auditors verify that these laws and regulations are being implemented.

- **High-risk audits.** For some events the consequences of failure are unacceptable. These include the operation of airplanes and submarines, and the launching of rockets to the moon. A complete and thorough audit of the finished product is necessary before it is activated or placed into service. Auditors check inspection records, craft qualification records, design review records, and other forms of proof.

- **Registration audits.** The conformity assessment program was developed several years ago to promote international trade. Before a ship of grain was unloaded, an accredited laboratory would analyze the cargo to certain agreed specifications. This gave the buyer confidence that the grain was acceptable—before unloading the whole ship. When the first ISO 9001 standard was issued in 1987, the conformity assessment concept was applied to quality management systems. (It had been tried earlier in the military and nuclear sectors, with limited success.) Independent and accredited firms are hired to assess the compliance of suppliers to the new standard. Multi-lateral agreements promote the acceptance of results across international boundaries.

Is it *compliance* or *conformance?* While the terms are used interchangeably, a purist would say that *conformance* is associated with something tangible. An item is *conforming* if it meets the form, fit, and functional requirements of the specification. If it passes inspection, it is *conforming*. In the industry, a *certificate of conformance* declares that the item possesses desired physical characteristics. *Compliance* to requirements adds another dimension. Not only does the item possess the desired physical characteristics, but it was also made using specified processes. A *certificate of compliance* says that the rules were followed in making the item or delivering the service. In this text, I will use the term *compliance audit*, as it is more comprehensive.

Compliance audits are designed to give assurance that activities have been performed properly. By their very nature, they are reactive (not proactive). One does not question the rules. One only looks for compliance to those rules. As with inspection, these audits are binary—pass or fail. Either the rules are being followed or they are not.

SHORTCOMINGS OF THE COMPLIANCE AUDIT

The compliance audit is high in evidence but low in judgment. Often, the results are presented as a completed checklist of observed conditions. Inspection is never perfect. Neither is a compliance audit. As a snapshot in time, the compliance audit says, "At this time, these conditions are being met. It's unknown if this will continue." Of course, we can increase the probability of being correct through rigorous and scientific sampling.

The compliance audit does not test the ability of the rules to achieve the organization's objectives. The auditor assumes that the rules are good and leaves such analysis to others—to be done during the annual management review or as part of the corrective action response to an unsatisfactory condition. There are many times when this approach is correct.

Compliance audits tend to discourage innovation. This is not totally bad, as there are times when you don't want innovation. For instance, would you really want the operators of a nerve gas incinerator to innovate on their own without consulting the engineering experts? The Three Mile Island nuclear plant incident in 1978 was the result of independent operator innovation to a set of unrehearsed conditions. When I was a young Naval Officer, an Admiral told me to operate the submarine in strict conformance to the procedures he and his staff had approved. Innovation (on my own) in this instance could have been quite dangerous. In certain high-risk and high-cost situations, a great deal of energy has gone into developing methods that work and innovation is not welcome.

However, most business and government operations are not high risk. Innovation is vital to their success. Any organization that continues to do exactly as it did before will soon be buried by the competition. Compliance auditing (by itself) will not serve the needs of most enterprises unless there is an incredibly strong corrective action system to address reported shortcomings.

Sometimes the planning part of the Plan, Do, Check, Act (PDCA) cycle is not as good as it should be. Requirements are not clearly defined and the "big honking manual" doesn't really say much. Often, this is because the control methods haven't been defined yet. Other times it's because the organization may wish to avoid auditor scrutiny. Regardless of the reasons for this lack of definition, the compliance auditor does not have a charter to say, "These are stupid rules. They don't say anything."

We are rapidly moving to a society where the team is more important than the leader. This shift in power is being felt in factories, offices, and shops around the world. Because of the binary nature of compliance auditing, teamwork is discouraged. It generates antagonism between those evaluating and those being evaluated. It results in finger pointing. Because they are not a part of the team, compliance auditors may not feel the need to study and prepare for the audit. They may be tempted to merely grab a checklist, look at what was examined last month, write the report before lunch, and fill out nonconformance sheets for the rest of their afternoon. We need something more than just compliance audits.

PERFORMANCE AUDITS

A performance audit looks at three things:

1. Compliance to the rules
2. Effectiveness of those rules for use
3. Suitability of the rules for achieving an organization's goals

The *compliance* part was discussed previously. An *effective* control is one that works as designed. Is it technically correct? Does it communicate in a meaningful way to the end user? Is it accessible? *Suitability* examines the ability of the controls to accomplish the task in an efficient manner. Do they have the breadth and depth to get the organization from here to there? Are they the right set of rules?

A performance audit looks for efficiencies and business results. We recognize that all is not perfect. Sometimes, we do the best we can with the resources available. In a performance audit, the rules are challenged. The underlying principles driving those rules are accepted and not challenged.

The earliest efforts at examining compliance, effectiveness, and suitability were done by the corporate internal auditors and called *operational audits*. Larry Sawyer was a champion of these audits in the mid-1970s. Ten years later, we came up with the term *management audits*. Others call this a *value-added audit*. In the second edition of this book, I used the term *management audit* out of deference to original works published by Leonard,[12] Sayle,[13] and Mills.[14] I have since concluded that too many people focused on the word *management* and got confused.

This type of auditing goes beyond compliance (see Table 1.1). It first requires a deep understanding of the controls that are desired. It then examines the many methods being used to achieve those controls.

Table 1.1 Compliance audits and performance audits.

Compliance Audit	Performance Audit
Requirements are set	Requirements are questioned
Focus is on stability	Focus is on business results
Practiced by 1st, 2nd, and 3rd parties	Generally performed only by 1st party
It is well known	Not well known

Building on the foundation of compliance auditing, data are gathered in the field. These binary data bits (observations) are not yet ready for publication. They must be analyzed to determine if desired results are actually being achieved. Are procedures user friendly (effective)? Do established systems have the breadth and depth to get the job done (suitable)? As you can imagine, all of this thinking and analyzing is hard!

It is interesting to note that a performance audit must first gather compliance data. You must have facts to analyze. Sometimes, you need a smaller quantity of data for a performance audit, but the variety will always be greater. You need to explore patterns and the reasons why things happen. The *number* of change orders may be of greater importance than the *content* of the original document being revised.

PERFORMANCE AUDIT APPLICATIONS

Performance audits are most appropriate for internal use. You have control over your own corporate destiny and the resources being used. You make market decisions. By analyzing patterns and connections, internal auditors can determine the causes of the observed nonconformance. Internal auditors usually have greater access to cost and production data. They can identify production inefficiencies and market trends. In a way, this is a form of consulting. The auditors present processed information to management in such a way as to generate excitement and the desire to change. It comes from within. The auditors are now team members and problem solvers.

Performance audits can also be applied externally to supplier relationships. In most cases, this is harder than the internal audit. The difficulty may be due to lack of trust, unavailability of information, geographic separation, or all three. Unless supplier partnership programs are present, performance audits are impossible to implement. Audit scores, while useful for making an initial purchase decision, become less meaningful in a performance audit environment. Rather, the emphasis is on business values, relationships, and trust. These are subjective items and difficult to score.

In certain circumstances, performance audits can be applied to regulatory or award relationships. The commercial nuclear power industry in the United States is a good example. The future of nuclear power generation was in serious jeopardy. Wise regulators realized that the traditional and adversarial methods of slash and burn would no longer work. Government inspectors needed to do more than write traffic tickets and impose fines. They were trained to analyze the underlying performance and management of the regulated utilities. The U.S. Federal Aviation Administration is moving in this same direction for aircraft manufacturers. Examiners for the Malcolm Baldrige National Quality Award are also taught to conduct performance audits. These auditors look at all three issues: compliance, effectiveness, and suitability.

Although this text will concentrate on quality audits, the principles apply to any type of management control system. Management is the control of resources. The goals of quality, safety, environmental stewardship, and efficiency are all driven by the same set of rules: define requirements, produce to those requirements, monitor achievement of those requirements, and continuously improve on the requirements. This is the Plan-Do-Check-Act (PDCA) approach captured in much of the literature.

PRODUCT AUDITS

Audits may also be classified by scope, as product, process, and system audits. A *product audit* is quite similar to an inspection, where the completed item or task is examined to required characteristics. Sometimes, the finished item is even destroyed, as various characteristics are measured. Paperwork associated with the building of those items is also examined. These "out-of-box" audits are performed mainly in the electronics industry and appliance manufacturing. It is quite common to pull a box off the line and inspect the contents from the consumer's perspective.

Hospitals and hotels do quite a few product audits. The "mystery shopper" from corporate headquarters will check into a hotel and examine the experience as a guest. This mystery shopper will look for dust in the rooms, clean linen on the dining tables, and functioning door locks. The "product" being audited here is actually a service. In the regulated industries, especially medical devices and pharmaceuticals, record packages are used to prove compliance. Audits of these packages are done to make sure all the records are complete and ready for outside scrutiny.

Product audits require considerable resources. The return on the resource investment is often quite low. They focus on completeness of finished goods and services and do not require extensive training for the auditors. Their usefulness is limited.

PROCESS AUDITS

With the release of the revisions to the ISO 9000 family of standards, there is increased interest in the process approach to manage an organization. Quality Management Principle No. 4 states, "A desired result is achieved more efficiently when activities and related resources are managed as a process."[15] This increased attention to processes naturally leads to increased attention to process auditing. Yet, many approach the process audit as if it were a small system audit. Auditing the processes is not the same as process auditing. There are similarities in the two forms of the audit, and there are fundamental differences.

Product, Process, and System

Products come from processes. Every organization performs a series of steps to accomplish its mission. Those products can be tangible, such as a new car or a candy bar. They can be intangible, such as a pleasant shopping experience. They can also be machine instructions, in the form of software bits and bytes. The ISO 9000-2000 standard refers to these as the four product categories of services, software, hardware, and processed materials.[16]

A *process* is an action. It transforms something from one state to another. The process can be an activity, such as painting a part. The process can also be cerebral, such as analyzing data. Something comes in and it changes. The ISO 9000:2000 standard defines a process as "a set of interrelated and interacting activities which transforms inputs into outputs."[17] Two items are required for a process: an action (verb) and an object (noun).

A *system* is a group of processes all working together to achieve a common goal (see Figure 1.2). We can have "factory" systems, such as the generation of electricity. The heating system in a home is another example of a factory system. It uses a number of processes (sensing temperature, creating heat, distributing heat, and cleaning air) to make the house comfortable. We can also have "management" systems, such as the control of purchased items. Each of these systems has processes working together. The relationships between product, process, and system appear many times in the quality sciences (see Figures 1.3 and 1.4).

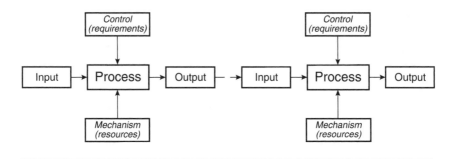

Figure 1.2 System: Processes working together to achieve a common goal.

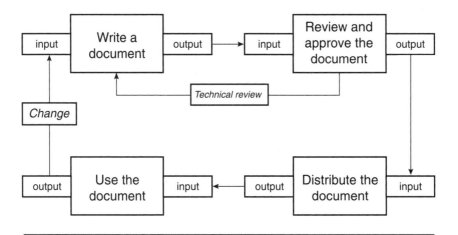

Figure 1.3 Quality management system processes (document control).

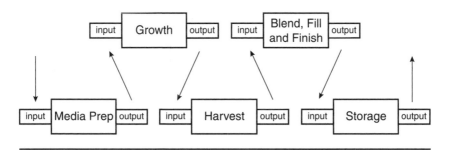

Figure 1.4 Factory processes (bioengineering).

Universal Process Forces

Methods, machinery, manpower, material, measurement, and environment affect all processes. These are often called the *universal process forces* (Figure 1.5). They had their start in the series of lectures published by Kaoru Ishikawa.[18]

Methods are the instructions we provide to the operator. They can be simple, such as a note to pick up milk from the store on the way home. They can be complicated, such as the procedure for installing an air lock on the international space station. Often, these are called *documents*. They are written before the task.

Machinery refers to the equipment used to perform the task. The tools must be capable of performing the task. They must be set up correctly and they must be sharp.

Manpower (and womanpower) refers to the human element. Operators must have knowledge, training, and experience to accomplish their tasks. They must be physically capable of doing the work. They must be able to reach the shelves and scrub the counter.

Material deals with the stuff coming into a process. It must possess certain characteristics if the process is to be successful.

Measurement includes both the data that are taken and the influences that measuring (itself a process) has on the activity being studied. Typically, we want to know what data are being taken and what we do with that resulting information.

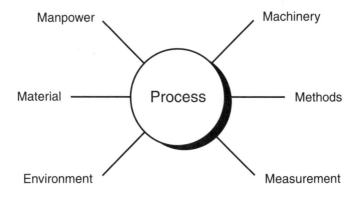

Figure 1.5 Universal process forces.

Environment refers to the outside influences on a process. Physical conditions, such as dust and radiation, can change the outcome of a process. These outside influences can be wanted or unwanted, and they must be controlled.

Overview of Process Audits

Process audits are short but intense. Rather than examine entire systems within or across the facility, you look at only a single process. The process audit examines an activity to verify that the inputs, actions, and outputs are in accordance with defined requirements. The boundary (scope) of a process audit should be a single process, such as marking, stamping, cooking, coating, or installing. It is very focused and usually involves only one work crew.

Many organizations refer to a process audit as a surveillance or a mini-audit to distinguish it from the much larger system audit discussed below. Given the right preparation, you can complete a process audit in about two hours.

A process audit should not be a one-time event. You need several data points to analyze for patterns and trends. You need a history of examination before you can pronounce the process ideal and move on to another process. You examine the process on the first shift and write a brief report. Next week, you examine that same process on the second shift. Next week, you examine that process on a different line. After a number of short process audits, you have sufficient information to draw conclusions.

Process audits may be for compliance only or they can address performance issues. Generally, it is easier to initially focus only on compliance. After the bugs are worked out and people are comfortable with the concept, you can move to performance auditing. Remember that even a performance audit requires compliance data.

You can use process audits as a trouble-shooting tool to examine product issues. Often, the cause of a problem is a bad process. An implemented process audit program is an ideal way to meet the continual improvement requirements of ISO 9001-2000.

SYSTEM AUDITS

A system is a grouping of interrelated processes, all working together to achieve a common goal. In your home, you have a heating system for cold winter days. The thermostat on the wall performs a sensing process. The gas burner or electric coils perform the heating process. The blower motor and fan distribute the heated air to the rooms. The filters in the air ducts perform a cleaning process. They must all work together if your home is to be comfortable.

We have educational systems, with many processes to teach our children. We have software systems, with input, subroutines, and display processes that (sometimes!) work. Of course, we have management systems. Management systems can be further divided into typical business activities with their associated processes. These include quality management systems, environmental management systems, safety and occupational health management systems, and financial management systems. All systems have linked processes, which must work together. The output of one process becomes the input of another process.

There are physical processes that accomplish the actual work. These are factory processes, such as bending, assembling, medicating, washing, and cooking. There are also management processes to control the environment in which the work is done. These management processes are also known as *controls*. A system audit evaluates the application of those interrelated (system) factory processes and management controls within the organization.

A *system audit* will audit the processes (and controls). It is at a higher level than process or product audits. System audits take longer and cover many different applications. A system audit examines an enterprise on the macro level, whereas product and process audits examine activities within that enterprise on a micro level.

System audits, by their nature, will generally cover many activities, both factory and management. They often cross organization, process, and product boundaries. Examples include one or more of the following:

- Product lines
- Process areas
- Functional departments
- Quality systems
- Manufacturing locations
- Customers
- Specific projects
- Time

A system audit might examine the maintenance system, the training system, the quality circle system, the drawing control system, or the order entry system.

A *horizontal audit* will look at the application of processes and controls across several functional groups. It gives us a good understanding of the way common rules are implemented across the enterprise. A horizontal audit is good for analyzing consistency.

A vertical audit will look at the application of several processes and controls within a single unit. It allows us to see if all the various rules are working together in an efficient and effective manner.

You should have a mix of both horizontal and vertical system audits within your organization.

SIX KINDS OF AUDITS

By using these categories, one comes up with the six kinds of audits shown in Table 1.2.

For best results, your internal audits should be a mix of about 75 percent process audits and 25 percent system audits. As you might imagine, process audits will nearly always be internal audits. The exception would be when a true customer-supplier partnership relationship exists. Suppliers might be having difficulties beyond their problem-solving capabilities. In the spirit of cooperation, they could ask you to perform a series of process audits on their activities. This would probably be a one-time series of process audits.

Third-party (conformity assessment and regulatory) audits are always system compliance audits. They look at the products (both goods and services) and processes (both factory and management) during their visit to determine compliance with system requirements.

Table 1.2 Six audit categories.

	Compliance Audit	Performance Audit
System Audit	Consistent implementation of a defined system. Promotes stability.	Ability to achieve organizational goals. Promotes change.
Process Audit	Performance of the ability in accordance with defined processes.	Ability of the processes to achieve desired characteristics.
Product Audit	Production of goods or services to defined requirements.	Suitability of the goods or services for intended use.

AUDIT DEFINED

The joint international quality and environmental auditing standard, ISO 19011-2002, *Guidelines for quality and/or environmental management systems auditing,* defines an audit as:

> A systematic, independent and documented process for obtaining audit evidence and evaluating it objectively to determine the extent to which audit criteria are fulfilled.[19]

The Institute of Internal Auditors has defined internal auditing as:

> An independent, objective assurance and consulting activity designed to add value and improve an organization's operations. It helps an organization accomplish its objectives by bringing a systematic, disciplined approach to evaluate and improve the effectiveness of risk management, control, and governance processes.[20]

Auditing may be thought of as the process of comparing reality with requirements. This comparison results in an evaluation to the stakeholders or interested parties. Managers want to know if their requirements are achieving the necessary controls. Stockholders want to know if the company is being efficiently run. Regulators want to know if laws are being obeyed. Auditors provide us with that information.

MANAGEMENT PRINCIPLES

Regardless of the goods or services produced, all management systems include four fundamental activities.

1. **Planning.** The activities to be performed should be planned before they happen. Responsibilities must be set so that accountability and ownership of resulting performance is established. The identity and needs of the customer should be defined. Requirements should be specified in written documents that are used to describe the work activity or products ordered. All the requirements and documents become the base against which quality is measured.
2. **Performance.** The action should proceed as planned. Records should be kept so that measurement can take place. Those performing the tasks should be given the proper tools and training to accomplish the job as specified.
3 **Measurement.** The success (or failure) of an activity needs to be measured against some accepted standard. Tools used include inspection, surveillance, audit, appraisal, evaluation, and review. All involved in the activity should be aware of the quality as measured. Feedback from the customer is vital to success.

4. **Improvement.** Measurement data will show where plans are not perfectly implemented. Problems must be corrected and the process improved. Managers and workers can share concepts for improvement, but the ultimate responsibility for such improvement rests with those in charge. Changes should be communicated to the internal and external customers.

These are the fundamental building blocks for any management control system. Often referred to as the PDCA cycle (Plan-Do-Check-Act), these blocks are used to improve the operations (see Figure 1.6). The audit is a tool to implement the last two (check and act) activities. There can be no audit unless requirements have been developed. Likewise, some activity must have taken place in order to measure the implementation of those requirements.

FUNDAMENTAL RULES FOR AUDITING

In order to provide others with the knowledge they desire, quality audits must follow these four basic rules:

1. Audits provide information for decisions.
2 Auditors are qualified to perform their tasks.
3. Measurements are taken against defined requirements.
4. Conclusions are based on fact.

Each of these basic concepts will be discussed in greater detail in subsequent chapters.

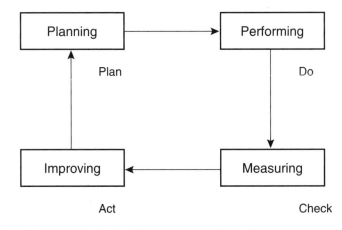

Figure 1.6 Plan-do-check-act cycle.

MAY AUDITORS SAY GOOD THINGS?

Yes. While it wasn't always permissible, current practice is to allow auditors to say good things as well as bad things.

For most of the 20th century, external financial auditors were not allowed to embellish their serious reports with a judgment of management practices. "Just tell me if we are following required accounting practices," was the request. As businesses started to employ internal financial auditors, some of this judgment crept in as a desirable practice. Operational auditing added even more judgment.

The early days of quality auditing reflected the original charge to report just the facts. This desire to report only objective facts came from the serious business climate of the times, plus the adversarial nature of customer-supplier relations. If you told your contractor good things, they would use it against you later when they were called to task.

Government regulators were faced with the same situation. The regulated firm's legal counsel would use positive statements to rebuff proposed fines or citations. It became policy to never mention anything good in a field report.

This all changed in the early 1980s, as competitive and business pressures forced both industry and government to revisit this philosophy. We remembered what the psychologists had said, that people and organizations respond more to positive news over negative news. Good is more powerful than evil!

On an individual level, you should tell people when they perform their job correctly. You instill a desire to continue the good work, especially since you are an outsider and often seen as the expert. Take care not to overdo it, though. Praise when praise is due.

On the organizational level, we expect people to be doing what they promised. You should not offer praise for doing what is expected. If the practice is above the norm and at the world-class level, then praise is appropriate. If you want to encourage others to adopt the same approach, then a little bragging will go far.

Even if things are not wonderful, it's OK to say everything is OK. You are not receiving a bounty payment for each finding you issue.

A DIFFERENT PHILOSOPHY

To be useful, audits must be performed and presented in a meaningful fashion. We must work *on* the system as well as *in* the system. In order to change practices for the better, audit results must be in business terms and appeal to the interests of the various stakeholders. Do they really care if six 5391 Forms are missing the Shift Supervisor's signature? So what? If, however, your audit is performed such that a projection of the continued practice of not recording reviews shows that the quality of the maintenance program is or could be adversely affected, then the responsible managers can take steps to correct the situation. Or perhaps this was just a bad day for an otherwise excellent employee, and represents no real threat. Folks can then turn their attention to more important matters.

A different perspective for audits is needed. Instead of examining past conformance to requirements and regulations in minute detail, you can use current performance to project future actions. It is better to avoid dwelling on mistakes of the past. They can never be changed. A backward-looking view cannot achieve the goal of improved performance within the organization being examined. It will only lead to antagonism and fighting. This is because people are powerless to change the past. They become frustrated and strike back, usually at you. Instead, use past practices to predict future performance, which can be changed.

Modern quality audits should be a combination of compliance and performance evaluations. Using defined and agreed-to measurement criteria, the audit report will tell us whether controls:

- Exist and are adequate
- Are being implemented
- Really work

The only way to successfully meet these needs is to thoroughly prepare for the audit, conduct the evaluation with a high degree of professionalism, and present the report in terms meaningful to the intended audience. Then your customers, using the information presented by the audit report, will be able to make changes to improve future performance.

ENDNOTES

1. Lawrence B. Sawyer, *The Practice of Modern Internal Auditing,* 2nd ed. (Altamonte Springs, FL: Institute of Internal Auditors, 1981): 3.
2. *Specification of General Requirements for a Quality Program,* ASQC C1-1968, ANSI Z1.8-1971 (Milwaukee: ASQC Quality Press, 1968): 3.
3. *Standards for the Professional Practice of Internal Auditing* (Altamonte Springs, FL: Institute of Internal Auditors, 2001).
4. *Government Auditing Standards* (Washington, D.C.: U.S. General Accounting Office, 1999), online at www.gao.gov.
5. *Generic Guidelines for Quality Systems,* ANSI/ASQC Z-1.15-1979 (Milwaukee: ASQC Quality Press, 1979).
6. *Quality Audits,* CAN3-Q395-81 (Rexdale, ON: Canadian Standards Association, 1981).

7. *Generic Guidelines for Auditing of Quality Systems,* ANSI/ASQC Q1-1986 (Milwaukee: ASQC Quality Press, 1986).

8. *Quality Systems—Model for Quality Assurance in Design, Development, Production, Installation, and Servicing,* ANSI/ASQC Q91-1987 (Milwaukee: ASQC Quality Press, 1987).

9. *Quality Systems Auditing,* BS 7229:1989 (London: British Standards Institution, 1989).

10. *Guidelines for Auditing Quality Systems,* ANSI/ISO/ASQC Q10011-1-1994, Q10011-2-1994, and Q10011-3-1994 (Milwaukee: ASQC Quality Press, 1994).

11. *Guidelines for quality and/or environmental management systems auditing,* ISO Q19011-2002 (Milwaukee: ASQ Quality Press, 2002).

12. William P. Leonard, *The Management Audit* (Englewood Cliffs, NJ: Prentice Hall, 1962).

13. Allan J. Sayle, *Management Audits* (Milwaukee: ASQC Quality Press, 1985).

14. Charles A. Mills, *The Quality Audit: A Management Evaluation Tool* (New York: McGraw-Hill, 1989).

15. *Quality management systems—Fundamentals and vocabulary,* ANSI/ISO/ASQ Q9000-2000 (Milwaukee: ASQ Quality Press, 2000): ix, Introduction.

16. Ibid, 10 (product definition).

17. Ibid, 10 (process definition).

18. Kaoru Ishikawa, *Guide to Quality Control* (Tokyo: Asian Productivity Organization, 1982).

19. See note 11.

20. See note 3.

2

AUDIT PROGRAM MANAGER

ACCOUNTABILITY

Success is difficult in any organization without responsibility, authority, and accountability. The audit program should serve the needs of the organization and the audit program manager must make sure it does. He or she is accountable to senior management for audit success or failure. While some firms have tried to accomplish this accountability by committee, it rarely works. You need one person in charge of the audits. You need an *audit boss.*

The audit boss doesn't have to be from the management ranks, but usually is. Often, the audit boss is the quality coordinator or the quality manager. The audit boss could also be a plant engineer or a production coordinator. For third-party audits, the audit boss is the person in charge of the auditors within the registering company or the regulatory agency. For most small- and medium-size enterprises, the audit boss is not a full-time position. You do this along with all your other duties. Most companies have only one audit boss for both internal and external audits. If the number of supplier audits exceeds 100 per year, it is best to have a separate supplier audit boss. This might be the purchasing manager or the procurement quality manager.

While it is acceptable (and sometimes even desirable) for the audit boss to perform an occasional audit, too much is dangerous. As an audit boss, you contribute to the checks and balances. After a while, you are less likely to challenge your own performance. You may even spend more energy on excuses than corrections. The audit boss should perform no more than a fourth of the audits.

In addition to accountability for the audit program, the audit boss is responsible for two products: the audit schedule and the audit resources.

AUDIT SCHEDULE

An audit schedule guides the audit program through the year. It is a communications tool. It helps to assure that all areas are covered.

The audit boss will first solicit audit needs from the many functional groups within the firm. We can never audit everything we wish, so priorities must be set. Resources, such as people, money, and time, must be allocated. We must also consider regulatory and other external forces.

Over the years, some have come to the mistaken conclusion that all areas and operations must be audited annually. This is incorrect and it wastes your precious resources. Quality management system standards state that audits should be performed on a periodic basis, according to the needs of the organization. All areas and operations do not possess the same degree of importance. They must be examined to the three common business factors of cost, production, and risk.

You must first determine what areas, operations, and suppliers should even be in the audit program. You can't possibly audit everything. Then you determine the frequencies of those included areas, operations, and suppliers. Some areas deserve to be examined twice a year. Some can wait two years between audits. Three years between audits is generally considered the maximum time.

Working with senior management, the audit boss will develop a matrix of the areas to be audited and the frequencies of those audits. This information is displayed on a spreadsheet or table. It should be published as a controlled document to show legitimacy and keep it current. Internal audit schedules (Table 2.1) and supplier audit schedules (Table 2.2) are usually published separately. If you can get the plant manager to approve the internal schedule, there's a higher chance it will be implemented. Likewise, the purchasing manager should approve the supplier schedule.

RESOURCES FOR THE AUDIT PROGRAM

The audit boss is also responsible for the resources associated with the audit program. This includes people, training, space, time, and equipment. The audit boss then assigns specific audits from the published schedule to an audit team. Composition of the audit team will be discussed in

Table 2.1 Internal audit schedule.

Audit Areas	JAN	FEB	MAR	APR	MAY	JUN	JUL	AUG	SEP	OCT	NOV	DEC
Accounting & Finance												X
Corrective Action										X		
Document Control												
Marketing (CS & OE)											X	
Personnel Training												
Production (all lines)							X					
Purchasing Group			X									
Quality Assurance												
Inspection & Lab									X			
Research & Engineering								X				
Shipping & Receiving						X						

Table 2.2 External audit schedule.

Supplier	JAN	FEB	MAR	APR	MAY	JUN	JUL	AUG	SEP	OCT	NOV	DEC
Allen Mfg.										X		
Aphasia Antifoam												
Baker Bolts				X								
Columbia Cableworks								X				
Jones Lab Supply											X	
Orefield Plastics												
Paragon Chemicals					X							
Sampson Steel, Ltd.									X			
Smith Fabricators												X
Tennessee Timepieces							X					
Wonder Welding						X						

greater detail in the next chapter. Of course, the audit program should have a few written procedures to assure continuity and completeness. The audit boss is responsible for these audit procedures.

THE CLIENT

One of the confusing aspects of audit program management is the relationship between the client, the audit boss, the audit team leader, and the auditee.

The term *client* originated from the financial audit profession, where an outside financial auditor would examine accounting records for a corporation. The corporation paying for this audit was called the *client*. The client was the customer for this audit engagement. One of the partners of the auditing firm would assign auditors to perform the audit. The partner, acting as audit boss, would negotiate the audit purpose and scope with the client to assure customer satisfaction. At the end, the audit assignment was finished when the client accepted the report.

As we applied this financial auditing model to conformity assessment (third-party auditing) of quality management systems, we picked up the term *client*. The early Canadian CAN3-Q395 standard defined the client as, "The organization that requests the auditing organization to conduct the audit."[1] Nine years later, the Canadian definition was picked up in the international ISO 10011 auditing standard, written at the time mostly for the conformity assessment community. It remains essentially the same in the ISO 19011 auditing standard of 2002. Today, it is mostly the professional registration firms (and of course accounting firms) that use the term *client*.

In theory, a client could exist in an internal audit program. In larger multinational firms, a group manager might request a series of internal audits for projects within that group. The audit boss would develop a schedule of audits, assign auditors, and deliver reports to that group manager. The group manager would be the client. A similar scenario might apply to external audits on a number of suppliers, where the purchasing manager was the client.

Most firms do not have the complexity described above. The audit boss negotiates with all stakeholders in the firm to develop a schedule for internal and external audits. The auditors perform the audits for the audit boss, who delivers their reports to the auditees.

ENDNOTE

1. *Quality Audits*, CAN3-Q395-81 (Rexdale, ON: Canadian Standards Association, 1981).

3

PREPARATION

PHASES OF THE AUDIT

Auditing may be divided into four phases:

1. The *preparation* phase starts from the decision to conduct an audit. It includes all activities from team selection up to the on-site gathering of information.
2. The *performance* phase begins with the on-site opening meeting and includes the gathering of information and analysis of that information. Normally, this is accomplished by conducting interviews, watching activities, and examining items and records.
3. The *reporting* phase covers the translation of the audit team's conclusions into a tangible product. It includes the exit meeting with those just audited and publication of the formal audit report.
4. The *closure* phase deals with the actions resulting from the report and the recording of the entire effort. For audits resulting in the identification of some weakness, the closure phase may include tracking and evaluating the follow-up action taken by others to fix the problem and keep it from repeating. This is referred to as *corrective action.* Auditing and corrective action are separate but related systems. Sometimes, the auditors monitor corrective action. Sometimes, they do not.

STEPS IN THE PREPARATION PHASE

Between the time you receive an assignment and the time the audit starts, there are many things to be done to lay the foundation and properly organize the work. The experienced auditor probably does it routinely from habit. The novice tends to do a great deal of fumbling in an audit before getting down to the actual surveys and examinations. To minimize such fumbling, you should use the following nine steps for preparation:

1. Define the purpose of the audit.
2. Define the scope of the audit.
3. Determine the audit team resources to be used.
4. Identify the authority for the audit.
5. Identify the requirements for the audited activity.
6. Develop a technical understanding of the processes to be audited.
7. Prepare an audit plan and contact those to be audited.
8. Perform an initial evaluation of lower-tier documents to higher-level requirements.
9. Prepare work papers for the collection of data.

While each audit is likely to be different from the others, these steps are common to all, regardless of where you will be and what programs will be examined. Just as airline pilots use a preflight checklist to verify that all items have been accomplished prior to takeoff, you may need to check a list before your own takeoff. Such a reminder list is not designed to inhibit your creativity; it will merely make the planning easier. Any format will do nicely, as long as it contains the items to accomplish and some due dates. (The nine steps mentioned above would be the minimum.) Once the list is prepared, you may proceed with an assurance that important actions will not be forgotten.

PURPOSE

What do you and your customers want to achieve with the audit? The answer to this question is critically important to the success of an audit and, thus, improved performance. However, in order to define the needs, you must first define the customers.

When you perform audits, you have three basic customers, as shown in Figure 3.1:

1. The auditee
2. The audit boss
3. The organization

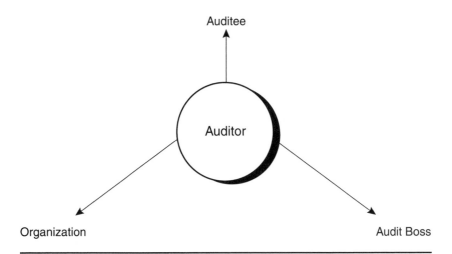

Figure 3.1 Customers of the auditor.

You must identify each of these three customers and determine their needs.

The people being audited are perhaps the most important customers. They will be working with you in the data gathering (fieldwork) efforts. Your actions and your product directly affect them. In official auditing terms, these people are called the *auditee.*

You must also serve the person who just gave you this auditing assignment. This is the audit boss. In official auditing terms, this person is called the *audit program manager.* (Refer to the previous chapter for more detail on the audit boss function.)

The final customer of the auditor is the organization as a whole. Practices, concepts, and even profits are all affected by your audit. You will have an influence on the functioning of your company or agency. For external audits of your suppliers, you represent your company to the outside world. They will see the company as you.

Of course, all three customers of the audit (auditee, audit boss, and organization) ultimately serve the external customer. When preparing for the audit, it is useful to picture the three internal customers and the external customer. Attach some names to these pictures. Then ask yourself, "What are their needs? How can I, the auditor, meet those needs?" This is a tall order, but very important to successful auditing.

As discussed in chapter 1, both compliance and performance audits address controls. The compliance auditor wants to know if the controls are defined and implemented. The performance auditor adds the additional considerations of effectiveness and suitability.

The probing of controls is at the core of every quality audit. It must always be addressed in the purpose statement for your audit assignment. The purpose of internal audits is normally associated with improving existing operations: reducing scrap, preventing lost time from accidents, shortening design to production cycles, and other business issues. The primary purpose of external (supplier) audits is to provide confidence in the quality of the goods and services delivered to your company, the purchaser. You must be assured that your supplier's internal control systems are working. Users of the third-party audit report are buying your expertise to evaluate the strength of the auditee's management. Notice that all of these thoughts ultimately return to the concept of comparing and analyzing actions to promises.

Performance audits must examine both the compliance with, and the effectiveness of, existing control methods. Your customers (users of the audit report) truly wish to know whether controls are being followed and whether those controls are working as planned.

This leads us to the first of four basic Rules for Quality Audits.

> 1. Audits provide information for decisions.

You, the auditor, act as an extension of the management function. You are the eyes, ears, and brain of management. Whether you perform audits internally or externally, you are being hired to think like a manager.

Once you have determined the purpose of the audit, write it down. Here's one for an apple packing plant:

> The purpose of this audit is to evaluate the adequacy and implementation of internal HACCP controls in meeting food manufacturing safety requirements.

Each audit should have a unique purpose; this is not something that is generated once and then recycled again and again. The generation of this unique purpose statement forces you, the auditor, to think about the task to be accomplished and the needs of your customers. Normally, the purpose statement is one or two sentences long.

SCOPE

Your next step in the preparation phase is to establish the scope of the audit. The scope establishes your boundaries and identifies the items, groups, and activities to be examined. Defining the scope also helps to make the most efficient use of limited audit resources, including the time resources of the people being audited. Production and staff assignments will always be adversely affected as you disrupt set routines.

The scope of an audit has a significant effect on the resources and time requirements for your audit. If the scope is too large, the audit cannot possibly be completed in a reasonable time. Conversely, too narrow a scope will waste valuable resources. Economics and personnel availability must also be considered when developing the scope. System audits that are greater than one week in duration for the performance (data gathering) phase are normally excessive. On the other hand, if the performance phase is less than a day, your return on investment (planning time and energy) is small.

Keeping track of the audit scope may be one of the more challenging tasks for the audit team. Often during the course of an audit, additional areas in need of examination appear that may be outside of the original scope of the audit. You must ask yourself whether the concern is important enough to pursue immediately, or whether it can wait for a separate examination at a later date. Consult with your team leader or your audit manager for suggestions. Generally, it's best to stick to the original scope, regardless of what develops. You will be perceived as more credible when you stick to the rules. Additionally, you probably lack the necessary preparation for that new area, leading to a poor job of investigation.

Does this mean that the audit team should ignore a serious deficiency, uncovered during the course of their audit, just because it lies outside of the current scope? Of course not. You should proceed as you would under a non-audit situation. Use the established methods already in place (for example, problem report, nonconformance report, or trouble desk) to report the condition to those managers that are affected. You have done your duty and can now proceed with the audit as planned. If the deficient area warrants additional, in-depth examination, ask the audit boss to place it on the audit schedule as a special audit.

THE AUDIT TEAM

In theory, the next step is to select the audit team, based on the purpose and scope just developed. In practice, the audit boss will use the known resources of the audit group in developing the audit schedule. A staff of two can perform just so many audits. Travel funds may limit the number of suppliers to be examined. Known resources will also affect your decisions on purpose and scope. The purpose, scope, and resources all affect each other.

Independence

It is often said that auditors must be independent of that which is to be audited. Going back to our roots of financial auditing, where an outsider was hired to examine the accounting books and records, this is theoretically achievable. In fact, ISO 19011-2002 states, "auditors are independent of the activity being audited and are free from bias and conflict of interest."[1] The idea is to allow the auditor to say the things that must be said, without bias or fear of reprisal. However, total independence is rarely achievable and will often lead to ineffective audits. A totally independent person knows little about the subject being audited. First-party (internal) auditors can never be totally independent, as the company they are auditing pays them. Supplier auditors cannot be totally independent, as supplier quality will determine the company's quality and thus success in the marketplace. Even conformity assessment auditors cannot be independent, as they are under contract to the company being audited. In a competitive environment, they must compete for registration business.

Actually, it is the audit *program* that is independent and not the *auditors*. The audit boss must be allowed to schedule audits in all authorized parts of the company, using the most capable team members available. The audit program must not be subjected to punitive action when reports say bad things.

Members of the Team

Continuous use of one-person audits is an invitation to trouble. To prevent your audit program from becoming a narrow interpretation of existing standards or methods, you need more than one auditor. No matter how well you plan or how clear the standards appear, the job will always require some interpretation. A single auditor will eventually steer those being audited down his or her path of goodness. While you may be blessed with a good deal of talent, eventually this single perspective will cause pain.

An audit team is defined as "one or more qualified auditors." While audits by an individual are allowed, the multiple auditor approach encourages balance. For the larger system audits you should have a team of at least two auditors. The person in charge of the team is called the *team leader* or *lead auditor*. Those on the team are referred to as *team members* or *auditors*.

Occasionally, you may find it desirable to use a subject matter expert (SME). The audit scope may include a particularly troublesome issue, requiring expert examination on a one-time basis. Be careful here. People will ask the expert for solutions. The expert will be tempted to provide those solutions. As we will show in the report section, this is generally not good practice and will often harm rather than help.

There is one additional category of team member: auditor-in-training. These are people assigned for the primary purpose of developing their audit skills through on-the-job training. Treat them as team members, but with additional attention and care. Auditors-in-training should be given real assignments and are expected to contribute to the effort like everyone else. They just need more watching.

Speaking of watching, audits performed on highly visible projects or in politically sensitive areas may have *observers* present. These are outsiders who represent special interests. Do not allow them to influence your audit in any way. They must not give direction. Pretend they are not there.

Auditor's Duties

The team leader is responsible for:

- Planning, organizing, and directing the audit
- Representing the team to the auditee and the audit boss
- Leading the team in reaching conclusions
- Preventing and resolving conflicts
- Preparing and completing the audit report

The team members are responsible for:

- Preparing for their assignments
- Gathering data and forming conclusions
- Contributing to the audit report

Team Size and Composition

A team of more than six members is a mob. Even the experienced team leader will find it difficult to control more than six. The ideal size for the system audit is two or three people.

One person will normally perform the smaller process audit. However, you should have more than one person performing a series of many process audits all around the plant. Some companies put their process audits under the direction of individual department managers. On any given day, one or two process audits will be occurring in each department around the plant.

While dedicated and full-time auditors sometimes exist in larger enterprises, most auditors are part-time. They perform audits along with a number of other duties. It is best to have a small core of people designated as team leaders. These are the ones who get to attend the training classes. They lead most of the audits and draw helpers as team members from throughout the facility. People from outside the traditional quality department functions should be considered as part of the audit program resources. It may be common for the team leader of a system audit to be a quality analyst or lead lab technician. However, your helpers can, and should, be drawn from both line and staff functions within the organization. You could start by looking back at the purpose and scope. Then invite some smart thinkers to join the team. These helpers might include training specialists, clerks, maintenance technicians, buyers, engineers, and even managers from another group. Other hourly employees from a related discipline may make ideal team members, as they often see the controls being examined from a different perspective and become champions for the defined controls after the audit is finished.

The makeup of auditors for the smaller process audits is easier to determine. All of the above-mentioned people are candidates for process auditors. Salaried, as well as hourly, people should be used for process auditing. The only serious limitation is the caution against vested interest.

Auditor Qualification

"Who should I use for this audit?" is an important question. The success or failure of your audit could depend on the composition of the audit team. Audits must be objective and unbiased. Auditors must have knowledge of the processes and how to audit them. These are the three conditions for qualification: objectivity, technical knowledge, and audit knowledge.

Objectivity

The audit team must be free of a vested interest in the area to be audited, so they can perform their duties in an objective and unbiased manner. They must not own the very thing being audited. It cannot be their creation. Their performance ratings cannot depend on the success or failure of the project to be audited. They cannot be in charge of the group to be audited.

Use of the word *team* here is deliberate. There are times when a member of the team could be very close to the design of the various controls being applied. Other members of the team are able to compensate for that closeness. Together, they possess the strength to see and report the truth, without the influence of ownership.

Technical Competence

Auditors must know the technical processes they are examining. They should understand common industry practices. They need to know what approaches are successful and where danger lies. While it is not necessary (or even desirable) for the auditors to be experts, they must know the processes and the language. Software auditors should know about code libraries and subroutines. Hospital auditors should know about trauma response. Auditors in a food plant should know about HACCP and bacteria controls.

Auditors should understand the bigger picture of how the systems function to produce the goods and services. They can achieve this knowledge in several ways:

- Review of previous audits of that area and the work papers in the file
- Instruction by someone who has the knowledge
- Reading manuals and procedures describing the operations

More detail on how to achieve this technical competence is provided in step six below.

The audit team, taken as a whole, should possess both technical and management system knowledge. Not only do we need to understand the technical processes used to produce the goods and services, but we also need to know the business processes under which it is happening. Interrelationships between functional departments are often as important as equipment operation.

The output of this process of becoming technically and organizationally smart is a flowchart. You have captured your reading, listening, and study on paper. You cannot perform a useful audit in an area until you can flowchart it. A flowchart of one or two pages of 10 to 20 boxes is fine. Use existing flowcharts as references, but draw your own. In doing so, you have to think. You are more likely to understand the activities about to be audited.

Audit Practices and Processes

Just as welders must know welding, auditors must know auditing. They should know about work papers, opening meetings, data collection, and problem identification. Auditing is a skill that is developed through reading, coursework, and practice. There are mechanical, intellectual, and emotional skills used by the auditor (see Figure 3.2).

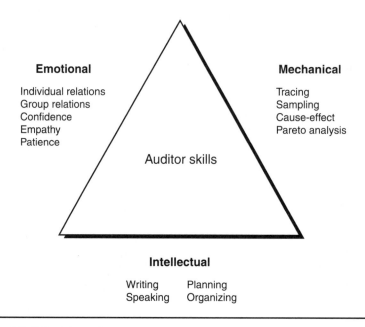

Figure 3.2 Skills of the auditor.

The mechanical skills deal with data gathering and analysis, such as:

- Sampling
- Tracing
- Cause-and-effect analysis
- Pareto analysis

Auditors constantly use the seven basic quality tools.[2] The brain uses intellectual skills to process data and communicate with others. These include:

- Writing
- Planning
- Speaking
- Organizing

Emotional skills are used in relationships with other people. These include:

- Individual relations (one on one)
- Group relations (one on many)
- Confidence (proceed knowing you are right)
- Empathy (understanding others)
- Patience (ability to handle adversity)

Of course, team leaders need to possess and demonstrate higher competencies than team members.

Certificate of Qalification

The three areas of qualification are:

1. Objectivity
2. Knowledge of the audited processes
3. Ability to perform audits as a leader or member

Every person performing an audit should possess a certificate of qualification. Someone has evaluated their skills and declared them to be competent. Each time you audit, expect others to ask you for your auditor certification papers; they have the right to expect decent auditors. Whenever you get audited, ask the auditors for their papers. There are three levels of qualification. Only the first is necessary in all situations.

Local Qualification

You are qualified to your own requirements. It is not necessary for everyone everywhere to use the same criteria. We have different needs and different cultures. The important thing is to set standards and meet them. One of the jobs of the audit boss is to define these qualification standards and document them in a local procedure. Topics to consider include:

- Technical understanding of the processes
- Understanding of how to audit
- Ability to communicate, both orally and in writing

It is common for the audit boss to qualify the team leaders and sign their papers. This qualification is evaluated annually for strengths and weaknesses. Team leaders should meet with their team members, explain the processes, and sign their papers. Team member qualification is only good for the single audit and expires when the audit is finished. Team members are always under the direct supervision of the team leader, so qualification is not a hassle.

Professional Qualification

While not necessary, it is good to have a few staff members certified by the American Society for Quality (ASQ) as *Certified Quality Auditors*. This adds professionalism to the audit program. It certainly makes the audit boss's job easier! The ASQ CQA designation says, "This person knows how to audit, in any environment, and has successfully passed a rigorous examination." Traditionally, about half of the people taking the exam fail on the first time try. It is tough! The exam is given locally by ASQ. Salary studies have shown that the market rewards the Certified Quality Auditor.[3]

Conformity Assessment Qualification

Registration and accreditation programs require auditors to possess specific knowledge and skills. They must thoroughly know the technical and management system standards for the industry. They must be able to perform audits such that other interested parties accept the results. Sometimes, international agreements require certain demonstrated audit abilities. These people most assuredly have papers!

SECOND RULE OF AUDITING

All of this discussion on team members and qualification leads us to the second of four basic Rules for Quality Audits.

---

2. Auditors are qualified to perform their tasks.

AUTHORITY

The next step in the preparation phase is to verify your authority to perform the audit. One reason for identifying this authority is to defuse the natural human reaction to become defensive when informed of a forthcoming audit. Some may even develop the opinion that they are being harassed. By specifying the authority for the audit to all involved parties (including your audit boss and other users of the audit), you confer legitimacy to the audit and remove (or minimize) those adverse feelings. Of course, another reason to verify your authority is to avoid wasting time preparing for something not authorized.

Your authority to perform internal (first-party) audits should reside in the document describing your quality management system. For most companies, this is called a quality manual. This document should first describe the product, process, or systems audits and define the authority of certain individuals or groups to perform them. It should describe your internal quality audit program. When you are reviewing the authority statements, be sure to verify that the area you wish to audit is included. Many companies will claim, "People are our most important resources."

Yet, the human resources group is not on the list of those functions to be audited. Sure, production is included, but have you included marketing and sales? These are all contributors to the quality of your product (as seen by the customers) and they should be audited.

Your authority to perform external (second-party) audits should reside in the purchasing agreements between you and the supplier. This is normally a contract or purchase order. Sometimes this authority is hidden in fine print on the backside of the contract document, often-times under the "rights of access" heading. This means, "We have the right to access your operations to check performance of this contract." Federal government agencies in the United States are required by the Federal Acquisition Regulations to include this authority in most sub-contract procurement documents.

For your really important suppliers, the agreement to perform con-tract performance audits should be stated on the front side of the pro-curement document.

What if the authority to do a supplier audit is not in the contract? (For older contracts, this is probably the case.) It is generally best to con-tinue preparation for the audit, but bring this deficiency to the attention of the responsible buyer, through the audit boss, so it may be corrected in the next contract change.

If your authority to perform internal audits is missing, you should not be doing audits yet. One of the requirements for an audit program is to have standards against which measurements are taken. If the audit procedure is missing, then other procedures are also probably missing. Write the other procedures first.

REQUIREMENTS

Requirements are the planned arrangements against which the perform-ance of an activity is measured. They are the *plans* part of PDCA. (See discussion of PDCA cycle in chapter 1.) Requirements and objective evidence are the two major inputs to the process of auditing, as dis-cussed earlier.

Recall that a *document* tells you what to do and a *record* tells you what was done. Documents are before and records are after. The requirements for an audit are always defined somewhere in documents, as shown in Figure 3.3. This is called the *basis* for the audit.

Without requirements there can be no audit. As we shall shortly see, these requirements come in a number of shapes and sizes. They can be internal and external, general and quite specific. When requirements are not defined, you use the data-gathering and analytical tools of the audit

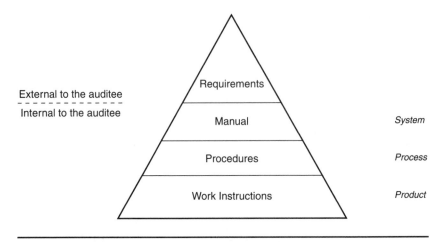

Figure 3.3 Document levels.

to perform *consulting*. The two activities are quite similar. There will be times when you are asked to use your audit skills for a consulting assignment. Enjoy it! This does not make you tainted and unfit for future audit assignments—except in that area. You now have a vested interest and should wait at least a year before examining the area as an auditor.

External Requirements

Documents, and thus our audit requirements, come in four levels. At the very top are requirements that come from outside the local organization. These cannot, and must not, be challenged. They come from many sources:

- International agreements, such as World Trade Organization
- National regulations, such as the U.S. Code of Federal Regulations (CFR)
- International consensus standards, such as the ISO 9000 series for quality management systems
- National consensus standards, such as the ANSI Z1.11 standard for training and education
- Industry codes and standards, such as the American Association of Blood Banks or the Institute of Food Technology
- Package labels and inserts, found on regulated products and devices

- Corporate policy, designed to provide consistent direction across the enterprise
- Customer requirements, reflected in the contract and purchasing specifications

Most of these external documents give broad requirements, such as "implement a system of internal audits" but do not give direction on how to accomplish these requirements. Some industry specifications, package labels, and customer requirements are quite detailed. Nevertheless, it is convenient to put all of these external documents into one category to remind us of the goal.

Local Requirements

The next level tells us how to apply the external requirements to our specific site. They describe our internal management systems for quality, environment, research, finance, and so on. These transition documents should be relatively skinny (about 50 pages) and are often called manuals. There may be several of these manuals, one for each section, department, or division. A binder filled with many procedures is not a manual. A level 2 manual should be narrative in its writing style, as if talking to your neighbor. It describes how the external requirements will be implemented at a particular site, facility, or location. Often, we use the manual as a marketing tool to impress potential customers. The detailed, step-by-step processes for accomplishing various tasks are reserved for the level 3 procedures.

Procedures describe processes. They give the step-by-step requirements for the job. Procedures must be clear, correct, and effective. They are job performance aids for a trained individual, not an unqualified outsider. Good procedures are less than 10 pages and have a flowchart to show the work steps. You will have many procedures available to audit, whether you are performing a process audit or system audit.

Procedures provide generic process instructions. There are times when you need details for a specific task. Work instructions are task or component specific. A recipe for peanut butter cookies (my favorite) would be a work instruction. Other examples include weld diagrams, inspection plans, and postal codes to call for tonight's telemarketing campaign. They give the details for a given process.

You should understand that not all organizations use this same nomenclature for their documents. That's OK. What's important is that:

- External requirements (including corporate if appropriate) are identified.

- The local *system* for achieving these requirements is described in some manner.
- There is a way of translating *system* theory into actual practice.

Documentation must be suitable for the organization and not the auditor. Your job is to see if those documents are achieving desired results.

These four levels of documents all have one thing in common: They provide direction on an activity to be accomplished. They are the first element in the PDCA cycle. Documents are descriptions of actions to be accomplished. They can be written on paper, published on a network, or even assembled as an example of the finished item. Don't confuse them with records, which are always generated after the event. Records are written or electronic descriptions of actions that have occurred. You will use both.

The manuals represent system-level documents. The procedures are process documents. The work instructions address product and service characteristics. This relationship of system to process to product will appear many times in your auditing activities (see Figure 3.4). Products and services are the result of processes, which depend on systems to tie everything together.

In order to provide assurances to your customers, you must audit more than one document. The larger system audits will examine the top

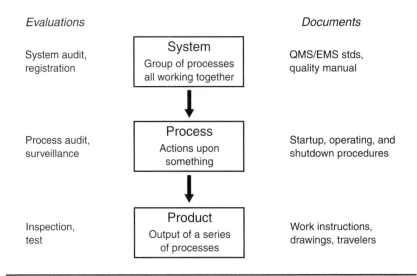

Figure 3.4 Product, process, and system relationships.

part of the pyramid (levels 1–3). The smaller process audits will examine the bottom part of the pyramid (levels 2–4). If you only examine conformance to a single procedure, you are doing a shallow and ineffective audit.

These documents represent the promises made by the auditee. In the overall model of auditing, they represent one of two inputs to the auditing process. They are the requirements. Their use in auditing is not optional.

This leads us to the third of four basic Rules for Quality Audits:

> 3. Measurements are taken against defined requirements.

In order to perform an audit, it seems reasonable that you must be aware of the various documents to be examined. Locate them. Ask for them. You will need to list them in the Audit Plan (discussion following). You will also need to study them before you can start the fieldwork.

Initial Informal Contact

At this point, you need to make initial contact with those about to be audited. Common courtesy requires you to let the auditee know what's planned. The days of surprise audits ended many years ago (except for waste, fraud, or abuse). You also need to make a list of the documents to be used for your audit. Soon, you will need to actually read and study those documents.

"How do I know what documents to use?" is a fair question. Trouble is, the audit boss doesn't have the answer. Only the auditee knows the requirements for the work. You will find your answers from the auditee.

This initial contact should be in person between you (as team leader) and someone in the group to be audited. If you can't do this in person, often the case for external audits, then use the telephone or e-mail. Don't be surprised if the initial reaction is panic! They probably forgot about your planned audit or may feel the urge to call in air support. Calmly explain that you are just getting ready. With preparation, perhaps you can ask better questions and not waste their time.

"But," you might say, "my supplier will not send me the manuals, much less any procedures." This attitude comes from the old style of auditing, where the objective was to find fault and assign blame. Previous auditors have probably hurt your supplier by hitting him over the head with his own manual. The natural reaction to such pain is to remove the source of that pain—the manual! You should explain that your purpose is to establish confidence. You need those documents to do your job. If proprietary material is contained in the documents needed, ask that it be removed before you see it. These hostile attitudes will not vanish overnight, but they will change over time.

Logistical details should also be explored for the supplier audit. These details might include security badges, proprietary agreements, suggested hotels, and other travel details. Mutually acceptable dates for the audit should be established so that the right people will be available during the audit period. Little good will result from an audit of a program that was scheduled when most of the participants were attending an important topical conference in Miami. A good rule here is to be firm but flexible.

For the smaller process audits, you provide this initial contact when the audit boss publishes the quarterly audit plan, discussed earlier. The folks already know that audits will be performed. They just don't know exactly when. You may show up on the first shift or the third shift, but you will show up. Of course, if you need to find some level 3 or 4 documents, then go to the shift supervisor or group leader before the audit and ask for them.

After all the discussions with your audit boss and team members and your informal contact with the auditee, you should have a fairly decent knowledge of the various level 1, 2, 3, and 4 documents to be used for the audit. Make a list of them.

UNDERSTAND THE PROCESS

You cannot perform an audit successfully (that is, improve performance) unless you have a technical understanding of the processes you will be auditing. By possessing this technical understanding, you will be able to navigate through the processes and ask intelligent questions. However, a caution is in order. Be careful if your team members are experts in the field to be audited. Although well meaning, such experts sometimes forget they are auditing and become consultants. This is a violation of basic rule number two (vested interest) and basic rule number three (audit against defined requirements).

Whether you are about to perform a small process audit or a large system audit, you must know the basic process steps and the areas or groups involved in those steps. You can get this knowledge by:

- Reading the notes of previous audits in that area
- Reading the manuals and major process procedures
- Talking with a trusted friend who knows about the area
- Exploring your supplier's Web site
- Reading the process maps and flowcharts

There are two additional methods for supplier audits that deserve caution.

A written survey or questionnaire is a common tool for evaluating potential suppliers. Define certain key controls that are desirable. Then ask the suppliers if they have those controls implemented. Sometimes, this approach is good for audit preparation. Key areas of interest are identified and the supplier provides some answers. This has merit if the size of the questionnaire is reasonable, perhaps 10 printed pages. The 50-page Standard Form 12 approach is burdensome on them and promotes laziness on your part. Seldom will one set of questions fit all suppliers. Finally, the focus areas of your audit will change over time, as the customer-supplier relationship matures.

Another way to understand the activity is to take a tour of the place. Watch the operations taking place and notice the location of major equipment. The tour is informal and short, generally without the rest of your team. What if you find something really bad? You have this natural desire to call home and report it. In doing so, you have started your audit—without a checklist, opening meeting, or even a team! You have totally destroyed the trust and respect building between auditors and auditees. Because of these dangers, think carefully before going on a pre-audit tour.

The best way to demonstrate (and clarify) your understanding of the processes is to flowchart them (see example in Figure 3.5). This is one of the seven basic tools[4] and will be used often in auditing. Know how to flowchart processes! If you can't flowchart, you will find it very difficult to audit.

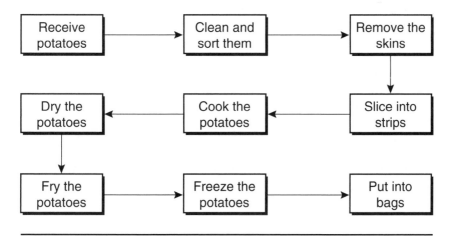

Figure 3.5 Example flowchart for fried potato processor.

Once you have a visual diagram of the processes on paper, you now know the answers to the following questions:

- Who does the job?
- What is the job?
- Where is the job done?
- When is the job done?
- Why is the job done?
- How is the job done?

These six words (who, what, where, when, why, how) will be used many times in the audit.

AUDIT PLAN

Now is the time to write down all of the information you have gathered for this upcoming audit. The term used for this is *audit plan*. It is a brief description of the various elements of the upcoming audit. An audit plan is not the same as an audit schedule. The *audit plan* tells us what will be covered in a particular system audit or sequence of process audits. It is a work instruction document. The *schedule* tells us what audits will be performed within a certain block of time.

The audit plan should be written on one sheet of paper. It should contain the following items:

- **Audit Title and Number**—This is for tracking.
- **Auditee**—The group or area to be examined.
- **Purpose**—Why are you doing this?
- **Scope**—What will you be examining?
- **Requirements**—This is your list of documents.
- **Organizations Affected**—These are the affected departments or subgroups of the auditee.
- **Any Interfaces**—These are interested parties. They won't be audited, but they have an interest in the planning or results.
- **Team Members**—Identify the team leader, helpers, subject-matter experts, and any observers.
- **Overall Schedule**—Identify the approximate times and dates for the opening and closing meetings.
- **Review and Approval**—You are the document owner. Your team members are the document technical (peer) reviewers. The audit boss approves it.

The audit plan for a system audit (shown in Figure 3.6) should be specific to that audit. To make things easier, put your first audit plan into

---

AUDIT PLAN #AQA-0306
Corrective Action (Adhesives)

PURPOSE OF AUDIT
Determine whether the department-level procedures conform to aerospace industry quality program requirements, and whether they are effectively implemented in the production of adhesive compounds.

SCOPE OF AUDIT
This audit will examine just the corrective action system. It will cover activities associated with the new ceramic adhesive production line since January of 2003.

ACTIVITIES TO BE AUDITED
Research and Engineering
Quality Control
Procurement
Production—Ceramic Adhesives

APPLICABLE DOCUMENTS
General Specifications for Aerospace Quality Programs (VSG 00376)
Acme Adhesives Quality Program Plan
Acme Adhesives Quality Manual, Section 7
Acme Process Assurance Procedure, No. 29
Acme Production Dept. Quality Manual, Section 7

AUDIT TEAM MEMBERS
James Red (lead), Susan Black, Lionel Blue, and M. Joe Green

SCHEDULE
Pre-audit meeting	9 A.M.	Oct. 6, 2003
Audit		Oct. 6–7, 2003
Post-audit Meeting	4 P.M.	Oct. 7, 2003

INTERFACES
None

AUDIT PLAN APPROVED: _____ Date: _____

Figure 3.6 Audit plan for system audit.

the computer. The next time an audit is performed, you can load that earlier file and just change the affected information. All the formatting remains the same.

The audit plan for a process audit (shown in Figure 3.7) should cover a series of process audits. This is normally a quarter's worth of audits.

AUDIT PLAN #SAF 03-03
Fire Extinguisher Maintenance

PURPOSE
> Determine if fire extinguishers throughout the company are being maintained in a constant state of readiness.

SCOPE OF AUDIT
> The audit will examine only portable, handheld extinguishers of 20-lb. charge and less.

ACTIVITIES TO BE AUDITED
> All functional departments within the plant perimeter and all work areas will be included.

APPLICABLE DOCUMENTS
> NFPA Std 329—General Requirements for Industrial
>   Fire Protection
> Acme Adhesives Policy 12—Fire Protection
> Safety Manual—Chapters 2, 3, and 10
> Extinguisher manufacturer's technical manuals

AUDITOR
> Rebecca Hoffmann

SCHEDULE
> Jan–Mar 2003: One audit per week, such that all department work areas are examined by the end of March.

INTERFACES
> Guardian Services Insurance local representative.

AUDIT PLAN APPROVAL: _____ Date: _____
>   Howard Grand, Manager, Plant Maintenance

Figure 3.7 Audit plan for process audit.

All of the above information is placed in the process audit plan, but it covers more than one audit. The schedule part of the audit plan would indicate frequency (for example, weekly, first Monday of each month, every other shift) rather than a specific day and time.

You and your team members prepare the audit plan. The audit boss approves it. This is one of the many checks and balances built into a good audit program.

Formal Notification

After the audit plan has been prepared, formal notification to the auditee is now in order. This is step seven in the preparation process. You send the *audit plan* as an attachment to the notification memo (internal) or letter (external). More and more, you will see the notification as an e-mail message, with the audit plan as an electronic attachment. Notification for the process audit takes place by the quarterly schedule updates. Maybe a month before the end of the quarter, send out the next schedule with the process audit plans attached. (If you perform several series of process audits, you need plans for each series.) Send out a separate notification before each system audit.

Since you want your audit to address management issues, the notification letter or memo should be addressed to the senior person in charge of the area to be audited. For internal audits this is probably the department manager or area superintendent. For an external audit this is probably the plant manager or president.

When performing an audit, you report to the audit boss. You are on temporary assignment to the audit boss. The audit boss is accountable for the actions of the audit team. So, the notification letter, memo, or e-mail should come from the audit boss. Even though you prepared it, the audit boss sends it. This keeps the audit boss accountable and involved in the whole audit program. Because an external audit involves contractual matters, the audit boss should give the notification material to the buyer or purchasing agent to sign the letter or send the e-mail message.

You (actually the audit boss or buyer) should send this formal notice at least 30 days before the audit starts. You will be better prepared if you don't wait until the day before the audit. It also gives the auditee time to get ready. This is the second of several extensions of your hand of friendship. (The first occurred when you informally contacted them about existing requirements.) You want to build trust and understanding between you and the auditee. The formal notification will help to build that trust.

EVALUATE DOCUMENTS

As discussed earlier, performance audits evaluate the adequacy of controls as well as compliance with those controls. Even a compliance audit cannot start with the assumption that *all* controls are perfect. You must look at the flow-down of requirements from the higher (general) level to the lower (specific) level (Figure 3.8). In doing so, you become familiar with the activities about to be audited and the strength and weaknesses of the controls.

Because you perform this evaluation at your desk, before the field-work starts, we call this a desk audit. It is step number eight in the preparation process. Document evaluation serves two purposes:

1. You see if high-level (system) concepts are picked up in work activity (process and product) documents.
2. You obtain a better understanding of the work activity so that the performance phase of the audit can be completed in an efficient and effective manner.

You should start from the highest-level document you have. (You obtained copies of these policies, standards, codes, manuals, procedures, and so on, earlier for the flowchart process in step six.) Break the document down into the basic control elements:

- Identify important processes.
- Obtain bids from pre-approved sources.
- Provide all assembly instructions to the workers.
- Develop an internal audit schedule.

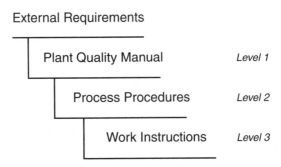

Flow-down of requirements:

External Requirements

Plant Quality Manual	*Level 1*
Process Procedures	*Level 2*
Work Instructions	*Level 3*

Figure 3.8 Evaluate documents.

Note that these are all action statements; they contain a verb and an object for that verb.

As you progress through the document, make a list of all these action statements. If you place them in a column down the left side of a page (or computer screen), it will be easier to record additional data to the right of each action statement. Now pick up the lower-level document and attempt to find the location, by paragraph number, where the action statement is addressed. Not all higher-level action statements need be addressed in a single lower-level document. In fact, they will probably be scattered among many lower-level documents. If you find the control item (action statement) addressed, write down the document and paragraph where you found it next to that control item.

If, after searching all your sources, you cannot find a control addressed, make a note of it next to that control item. If the procedure seems vague in its application of the control requirement, then mark your list accordingly. You will need to examine these areas in greater detail later in the fieldwork. Also, your study will identify specific records, forms, or reports that are used to implement the required action. These should also be noted on your list, along with identification of the person or place where those records should be available.

When you are finished with all level 1 documents, go to the level 2 documents and make another list of control items from that level. Attempt to find these new controls in documents further down the line.

What if you cannot find details on a higher-level control? You looked and looked, but it is not there. Don't give up yet. Go back to the auditee for more information. Your question, "Where is the guidance given to waiters on how to enter orders into the computer?" might well result in the answer, "Oh, I forgot to send you that instruction." While there are perfectly valid reasons for not documenting all activities, most likely, the detail is someplace. You just haven't found it yet. Plus, you are telling the auditee that you really are reading the material provided to you earlier.

What if you still cannot locate the implementation information? Add those items to your checklist for researching while you are in the field.

What if there are huge holes? Most of the implementation methods are not defined. Everything is vague. It is time to seriously question the wisdom of performing an audit of this chaotic operation! Remember the third rule of audits: audit against requirements. With no (or ill-defined) requirements, there can be no audit. However, you are not in a position to make such a decision. Only the audit boss can cancel or postpone a scheduled audit. This is not a decision made alone. The audit boss must consult with you, the managers of the affected areas, and other stakeholders.

All of this effort will lead to a much greater understanding of the way various activities are designed to work. When finished, you now have a cross-reference of the controls to be examined and the document locations of each. This will be of great value in the next step: writing checklists.

WORK PAPERS

Recall from the overall model of auditing presented earlier that there are two inputs: controls (what should be) and data (what is). We covered the controls and requirements earlier. Now, we need to spend some time discussing the data. In order to gather this data, you need to know what it is. Just as you should prepare a list of groceries to buy before you go to the supermarket, you should prepare a list of data to gather before you start your audit. Work papers help us to gather data and record it for processing.

This leads us to the fourth of four basic Rules for Quality Audits.

> 4. Conclusions are based on fact.

The team will be expected to examine all of the selected control areas identified from the various documents chosen for your audit. Additionally, a method is needed for organizing all of the information gathered during the course of the audit. Audit work papers will meet both of these needs. They serve as guides to each member of the audit team, in order to assure that the full scope of the audit is adequately covered. They also provide a place for recording the facts gathered during the fieldwork. Work papers, prepared before the field visit, are a time-tested audit protocol.

Forms of Data

As you prepare your work papers, you should be aware of the five types of data to be gathered in the fieldwork. An analogy might be the picking of flowers in order to make a nice flower arrangement. You go out into the lovely field (the auditee's work area) and pick some flowers (gather data). You place these flowers (data) into your basket (checklist). Then you take your basket of flowers inside to make a nice arrangement (audit report). No flowers—no flower arrangement. No data—no audit report. There are five kinds of flowers:

1. Physical properties
2. Information from your senses

3. Documents and records
4. Interviews
5. Patterns

Physical Properties

This is the measurement, inspection, or count of tangible items. Examples of physical properties include the following:

- Markings on computer data disks
- Temperature of a drying oven
- Sizes of file folders
- The color of a wall
- The layout of a work area

Make sure, however, that you are qualified to measure something before you report it as a fact. Physical properties are regarded as one of the most reliable types of audit evidence. They represent reality. Your audience will have little difficulty relating to these tangible things when they are presented in the final report.

Information from Your Senses

Throughout an audit, there are many opportunities to use your sight, hearing, touch, and smell to evaluate a wide range of situations. By watching an action being performed, you can determine how the system is actually being implemented. Occasionally, you might be able to smell or hear something, but normally your eyes will be the primary means of input. Often this is accomplished by asking the operator to demonstrate a particular action to you. Have the operator conduct a database search and watch the action. See how a form is actually completed by following the other party around as they complete the various steps. As you watch, you are continually taking notes of the specific actions and items being accomplished. You are also asking questions to test the performer's knowledge of the procedure steps. By using your senses (mostly your eyes), you base your report on direct observation of actual activities being performed. The report is more realistic than if you had limited yourself to just the paperwork.

Documents and Records

Documents are used to specify an action, while records are used to substantiate that something was performed and that it met requirements. Most important transactions and processes should be supported by a document. Often, records will be generated as a result of these controlled actions. So, there is a large volume of this type of evidence available to you. Records are the most frequently used source of information, but are also the most frequently abused. You must remember that all activities are not, and should not be, recorded on a piece of paper just to make the auditor's job easier. If it is not recorded, look for evidence elsewhere.

Interviews

This is the process of obtaining information from another person in response to your questions. The methods used for conducting interviews will be discussed in the next chapter.

Patterns

Comparisons and relationships among data points may be used as a means of isolating or highlighting certain activities. You may compare the way two groups perform the same task. Another example of this type of evidence would be to conduct a trend analysis on such things as the number of field support calls per month over the past year to determine whether the rate for a certain code version is increasing or decreasing. (This also allows you to determine if the code change made things better or worse.) Other examples of patterns include trend analysis (increasing or decreasing), percentages, and ratios. Actually, patterns originate from one or more of the above four forms of data.

Objective Quality Evidence

In the beginning days of financial auditing, one would gather facts, called *observations*. A financial observation might be, "The chart of accounts does not distinguish between long-term and short-term debt." The auditor would then draw conclusions (findings) from those observations. Quality auditors adopted this same model of forming conclusions from facts. Over the years, though, observations in our profession have morphed into a sort of mini-finding. As though the auditor is saying, "I can't quite write you up, but I believe this is wrong." Even though we always said, "This is not a violation," the implication was "You had better look at this or I'm going to make your life miserable."

To further complicate matters, the U.S. General Accounting Office describes *observations* as the data gathered when watching something happen.[5] (See the discussion on senses above.)

Many auditors saw this sorry state and stopped using the term *observation* in the mid-1990s. When work began on the ISO 10011 revisions and then the ISO 19011 document, the term was dropped. In its place, we first used the term *objective quality evidence*. With the work to combine quality and environmental auditing into one international standard, we now use the term *objective evidence*. These are the five forms of data described above.

Types of Work Papers

There are generally three types of work papers:

1. Procedures
2. Flowcharts
3. Checklists

You may find it convenient to copy an important procedure and highlight the important parts of that procedure. Take your highlighted procedure into the field and see how it is being used. Take notes in the margins of your procedure for later use in the report. For most audits, this approach is not sufficient alone. It is used to supplement other work papers.

You can also use a detailed flowchart or process map of the work area. This would not be your simple one-page diagram. Rather, it would show many inputs, outputs, and feedback loops. Use this diagram to see if the actual work is performed according to design, taking notes in the margins.

The most common form of work paper is the checklist, consisting of a series of questions with space to record answers.

Contents of the Checklist

There are certain criteria that any audit checklist should include, regardless of the audit subject or scope. Obviously, the checklist must first provide for clear identification of the specific audit topic or subject to which it applies, the organization(s) to be audited, and the audit dates. A unique reference number may be assigned to your audit and this, too, will be identified in the heading information of the checklist.

Remember that the main function of the checklist is to gather data. List the specific points to be examined in a logical order. The format by which this is accomplished will vary from office to office. Some choose to list the questions in a column down the left side of the page (see Figure 3.9). A center column for checking yes/no or sat/unsat follows. The right side has a third column for recording the objective evidence examined for that question. Others choose to simply list the questions on the page with an inch or two of white space between questions for recording notes and reference to objective evidence (see Figure 3.10). Any workable format is acceptable.

Audit Checklist 23-03				
Requirement	*Yes*	*No*	*N/A*	*Notes*
First question (reference)				
Second question (reference)				
Third question (reference)				

Figure 3.9 Columnar form style of checklist.

Audit Checklist 23-03

1. First question is written here, across the entire page, using word wrap. At the end of the question, the reference is shown in parentheses. The question is followed by blank space to allow for handwritten notes in the field.

2. The second question follows the first in a similar fashion.

3. The third question follows.

Figure 3.10 Free form style of checklist.

Each checklist question should address one piece of information. If you try to include many facts in one question, you will wind up confused and probably miss some of those reminders when you get to the field.

Checklist questions are not the open-ended questions to be discussed in the field; rather, they are the individual facts you will need to form conclusions. They must be precise. They must be measurable. They must be facts. To better accomplish this, try to phrase your checklist questions in yes or no form. This makes your questions binary, as opposed to the analog-type questions you will ask in the interview.

The questions should also reference the specific section of the document that established a particular requirement. These cross-references provide you with a handy reply to the question, "Where did that requirement come from?" They also force precision in the development of the checklist in the first place. This keeps you away from the temptation to make up your own rules.

One approach often used for the development of checklist questions is to separate each requirement paragraph of a particular standard into smaller, manageable bits, then to rephrase those requirements in the form of questions needing a yes or no answer. As stated before, these are intended as questions for you to answer after review of the procedures, completion of interviews, and examination of evidence. In other words, you must determine whether the group being reviewed does or does not meet requirements.

Most word processing software has built-in drawing capability. You can use this feature to place a simple version of the flowchart up in the page header. That way, you have a map associated with the questions. It's much easier to follow. Of course, you should put a section break every few pages, so you can insert a different flowchart at the top for the next portion of your checklist.

When preparing your checklist questions, you must be careful not to change the essential requirements of the document by careless use of similar words, as you have no authority for rewording a requirement to reflect your own bias or preferred way of accomplishing a task.

Collection Plan

It is often desirable to include a plan for the collection of specific evidence needed to answer certain checklist questions. What do you wish to look at? How many items do you want to sample? What are the criteria you will use to judge acceptability? These are the types of questions that can be addressed in a collection plan. Naturally, you won't know all of the places to look prior to the audit, but you should be aware of some.

Collection Plan Audit #INS 03-10						
Select six carpet samples from the last two production shifts:	1	2	3	4	5	6
1. Record the type of carpet.						
2. Record the color.						
3. Record the production run number.						
4. Was the sample at least 10 x 10 cm.? (SIM 3.2.5)						
5. Was the run number recorded on the QC inspection sheet? (SIM 3.2.7)						
6. Was the color test device calibrated within 48 hours of use? (Tech Man 6-1)						
7. Were inspection results available prior to release of the production run? (BMM 4-13)						
8. Were anomalies reported to the shift supervisor within 1 hour? (BMM 4-13)						

Figure 3.11 Collection plan.

The collection plan should provide you with space for recording the results of your examinations, including an identification of those people you talked with. As mentioned previously, some people prefer columns for entering data and interview results, while others prefer white space between individual questions. A matrix arrangement works especially well for collection plans (see Figure 3.11). You should use the format that works best for you, as these become your notes and the success of the audit may depend upon how well you can reconstruct an interview or record review.

Process Approach to Auditing

As you begin to understand the way processes function in harmony to form a system, you will find the process approach to auditing very productive. The activity linkages become clearer and the audit becomes more fun! Your report has more value when it relates to actual work being performed. (Please see chapter 1 for a discussion of processes and the general model of inputs, outputs, requirements, and resources.)

A drawback to the process approach is the additional time (and thinking) required for developing the checklist questions. Each organization has different processes to accomplish its mission. Some make cookies, some write software, and some build airplanes. Even the support processes of training, document control, and instrument calibration will vary from firm to firm. It is difficult to use (and reuse) a single checklist for all of these situations. A generic approach, however, is possible.

Take your flowchart from step six above and examine the process boxes. Each process will have inputs, controls, resources, and outputs, as shown in Figure 3.12.

1. Start on the left with the inputs. What controls exist here? Are input characteristics (form, fit, and function) defined and measurable? What communication channels exist? What handling actions take place? These are all valid checklist areas to consider. Of course, the questions themselves should be specific and relate to actual requirements.
2. Now, look at the control items above the process box. Where are requirements found? What procedures and drawings describe the activity? Are they the latest and greatest?
3. The resource elements are below the process box. This is how the process is performed. It is here that machine setups and maintenance activities become important. People skills and training are in this area.

4. Finally, the process output must be defined and controlled. Measurements are taken with calibrated equipment.

Repeat these four steps for each of the major processes on your flowchart. You now have a detailed checklist, or series of checklists, covering external and internal requirements. You have both generic and activity-specific control areas defined. You are ready for the process approach to auditing.

Standard Checklists

Some organizations like to use canned checklists, which, once prepared and approved, are used for all subsequent audits. By themselves, these standard checklists do not reflect how a particular department, factory, or branch office assigns responsibilities and authority. They fail to identify special features of a particular program that may be crucial to success. They only address some of the performance criteria, usually only the top level. Additionally, they allow the audit to proceed without site-specific preparation and thought. These standard checklists are fine for third-party registrars who do conformity assessment to a high-level

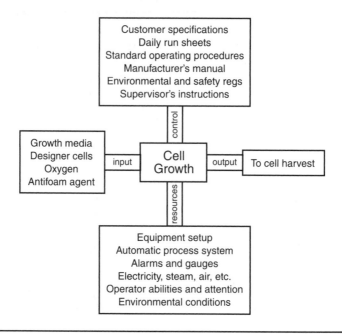

Figure 3.12 Process model for designer cells.

national or international standard. As the *only* work paper documents, they are less-than-useful for internal auditors. They just do not have sufficient detail for internal use.

However, a standard core of questions is useful. The audit boss may feel that each audit this year should examine equipment maintenance, for both office and factory processes. A standard set of a dozen questions will force every auditor to at least think about and examine the maintenance issues. You can then add or subtract questions from the baseline set. Previous checklists from other audits can provide you with a bank of potential questions for recycling. By placing these questions on a central file server, all have access and preparation time is reduced.

For the individual process audit, use a common set of questions for the current (three month) campaign. Use the same checklist for first, second, and third shift. Modify it slightly for the applications across the facility. The same questions are used each time the process audit is performed, until the campaign is finished. Then a new set of questions is prepared for the next process audit.

Checklist Assignments

All audit team members should prepare specific checklist questions appropriate to their individually assigned portion of the job. For example, one individual might be assigned to examine document control, another to control of the computer source code library, and a third to calibration of test instruments. Each individual would identify specific requirements applicable to the assigned area and enter them onto a checklist.

When finished with the checklist development, each team member should submit his or her portion to peer review. This serves as a check of thoroughness, proper logic construction, and absence of bias. Any qualified reviewer will do. This may be the team leader, another team member, or your group manager. The purpose of this review should not be to approve your checklist, but rather to subject it to a critical examination of content. This practice will lead to better checklists and thus better audits. Once done, you should record the review somewhere so that you may take credit for it. Usually, a signature and date at the bottom of the first page of the checklist is satisfactory.

History

In developing checklists and preparing for the audit, it helps to know the history of the area under review and how successful its implementation has been. You or someone else may have performed a previous audit in this or a similar area. If this is the case, you should review records of prior audits and identify from the records any specific area likely to have continuing or repeat problems. If the prior audit revealed noncompliance areas, you should determine the current status of actions that were taken to resolve those issues. Others may have closed out these items based on information that specific corrective actions were implemented. The new audit team should verify that these actions have remained in effect, and that they have been effective in preventing recurrence of the problem or noncompliance. Previous nonconformance reports and program assessment reports may also prove to be useful in identifying areas to explore.

In your review of past audits of your assigned area, you also want to note the strengths that were previously identified. One of the objectives of your audit should be to verify that these strengths have not eroded through changes in personnel, equipment, office reorganization, or many other reasons.

For external supplier audits, this may also be a good time to discuss the supplier's performance with the various stakeholders. They may have particular areas of interest that merit examination by your audit team. Also, these users are the ones that stand to gain the most from the supplier's improved performance, which is the goal of a second-party audit.

Add this review information to the audit checklist. This is another reason to avoid the use of canned checklists; they cannot be revised to account for additional information that comes from review of the supplier's history. The checklist is a constantly evolving document that is modified right up to the point of preparing the audit report.

SUMMARY

Here are the products of the preparation phase:

- An audit plan
- An audit checklist
- Completed logistical arrangements
- An initial evaluation of the formal (identified) controls
- A plan for the collecting of facts

The audit plan will identify the organization to be audited, the subject or purpose of the audit and its scope, the activities to be reviewed, members of the audit team, and the documents (requirements) applicable to the audit.

The audit checklist will identify the various items to be examined and the reference location for each requirement. It will show the facts you need to obtain during the audit. The checklist will contain space for recording both bad facts and good facts, along with space to record comments and notes regarding certain conclusions.

The auditee knows why you are doing this audit and what you intend to examine. You have mutually agreeable dates and a rough schedule for the fieldwork. You have copies of the various control documents and organization charts, along with additional procedures and instructions applicable to the audit. Travel arrangements, including hotel reservations, are in place.

From your review of the formal control methods (desk audit) and discussions with the users, you have identified areas of probable strengths and weaknesses in the activity to be evaluated. You have also prepared a plan for collecting evidence. With the audit plan and checklist in hand, and with the necessary arrangements made, you are well on your way.

ENDNOTES

1. *Guidelines for quality and/or environmental management systems auditing,* ISO Q19011-2002 (Milwaukee: ASQ Quality Press, 2002).
2. The *seven basic tools* include flowcharts, control charts, cause-and-effect diagrams, histograms, check sheets, Pareto charts, and scatter diagrams. See the June through December 1990 issues of *ASQ Quality Progress* magazine for more details on these tools.
3. ASQ annual salary survey published in December issue of *ASQ Quality Progress* magazine.
4. See Note 2.
5. *Government Auditing Standards* (Washington, D.C.: U.S. General Accounting Office, 1999), online at www.gao.gov.

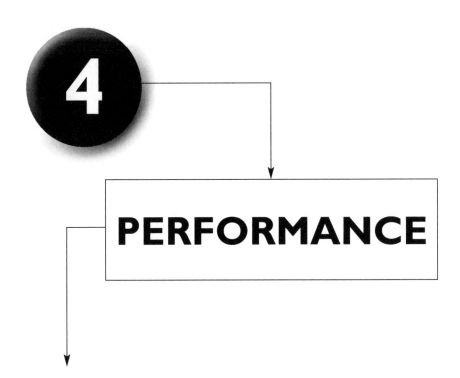

PERFORMANCE

The performance phase of an audit is often called the *fieldwork*. It is the data-gathering portion of the audit and covers the time period from arrival at the audit location up to, but not including, the exit meeting. It consists of the following activities:

- Meeting with the auditee
- Understanding the process and system controls
- Verifying that these controls work
- Communicating among team members
- Communicating with the auditee

We will discuss each of these activities in greater detail so that you gain a better understanding of the skills and mechanics needed.

OPENING MEETING

All audits must have some sort of opening meeting. This starts the data-gathering phase of the audit. The opening meeting, sometimes called an entrance meeting, is held soon after your arrival at the audit site. You should have your entire team at the meeting, so that they may be introduced. The audit team leader should take charge of the meeting and keep it brief. Most opening meetings can be completed in 15 minutes, if you know what you are doing and are adequately prepared. Prepare a meeting agenda and pass out copies before starting. (This will allow you, not the auditee, to control the meeting.) Elaborate presentations by the auditee only waste time. They are not needed. Remember that the more time spent watching a show, the less time you have for observing, checking, and questioning.

For the system audit, it would be ideal to meet with the manager of the area to be audited. If an assistant shows up, that is fine. If you only get a record clerk for the opening meeting, you should tactfully request someone from management. The smaller process audit is much less formal. Normally, a simple, two-minute meeting between you and the shift supervisor is sufficient.

Several things should be accomplished in the opening meeting. First, the purpose and scope of the audit should be restated. Those present may have only vague notions of what to expect, especially if this is the first audit experience. Usually, however, the group has been examined before and will have some idea of what will happen. As team leader, you should set the tone of the meeting by stating the purpose and scope in a clear and diplomatic fashion. Even though this information was already given in the notification letter, it may not have been received (or understood) by those present. The audit team and their counterparts should trade introductions, sometimes with a brief description of backgrounds and/or positions. Bring a stack of business cards and hand them out. This is also a good time to present your credentials.

You can form important judgments during the opening meeting. Are they relaxed or anxious, open or defensive? What seems to be the style of the group? Is the director alone and trying to dominate the meeting? Are the staff in attendance and do they participate? These observations will prove valuable in understanding people's reactions during interviews. They will also help when developing the tone of the report. You must impress upon those in attendance that you know the technical and business processes studied earlier. You can do this by asking confirmatory questions about the activities, such as "Will we be able to see the cleaning area and parts storage for maintenance of the hay bailers?"

You might want to solicit areas of interest from those at the meeting. Often, the response might be a desire on their part for you to examine a newly revised area, such as data reduction or records handling. They may also wish to know how they stack up against other organizations performing similar tasks.

Conversely, you may have areas of particular concern for this audit. If your research during the preparation phase has indicated a potential weak area, it should be mentioned. This will help your counterparts to prepare for your intense examination of those areas.

You should also pass out copies of your audit checklists, even if you sent them out earlier. This continues to emphasize your desire for cooperation and communication. It is a good idea for the team leader to have at least four copies available—one to give to the senior auditee representative as a display of respect, two to keep for the fieldwork, and another for someone to reproduce right after the meeting.

The most important part of the entrance meeting is to set the detailed schedule. It affects all the effort to come and allows the audit to proceed efficiently. A good way to accomplish this is to develop a matrix of team members and areas, with dates and times to be filled in at the opening meeting (see Figure 4.1). By discussing the information needs with your counterparts, you may be able to designate blocks of time for specified individuals. This accomplishes four important things:

1. It forces the audit process along.
2. It provides for good time management by those being audited.
3. It encourages a constant application of your resources over the entire audit.
4. It sends a strong message of cooperation to those about to be audited.

Audit Planning Schedule		
	Joe Maday	Suzy Swanson
Monday morning Monday afternoon	Entrance meeting On-site collection	Entrance meeting Remote collection
Tuesday morning Tuesday afternoon	Training (Admin) Lab testing	Remote collection Lab calibration
Wednesday morning Wednesday afternoon	Transfusion Records (Admin)	SOP controls (Admin) Audits and reviews
Collection Laboratory Transfusion Administration	Jeanne Burkhart Tom Campbell Betty Boop Dennis Sandmeier	First floor Basement Annex First floor

Figure 4.1 Detailed audit planning schedule matrix.

Such things as conference rooms, telephone access, safety considerations, hours of operation, and lunchroom facilities can also be discussed. Often, in the larger system audit, a guide or shadow from the auditee organization will be assigned to assist you and your team. The use of a guide is encouraged. This person is there to point you in the right direction and offer advice on who is responsible for a particular activity. They must not be allowed to provide you with all the answers, however. Your guide will usually take notes on what you are asking and examining. This is fine and contributes to the free exchange of information between auditor and auditee.

GATHER THE FACTS

The data-gathering process normally takes most of the time and effort in the performance phase of the audit. Recall from earlier discussions that the job of the auditor is to gather facts, compare these facts to requirements, process the information, and report the results to stakeholders. The checklist, prepared earlier, is the repository of these facts. It is a place to record the five types of data:

1. Physical properties
2. Information from your senses
3. Documents and records
4. Interviews
5. Patterns

Also remember that the fundamental questions to be answered by an audit are:

- Do controls exist?
- Are they being implemented?
- Do they really work?

Preparing for the audit will begin to answer the first of these questions, but you need tangible proof that your conclusions, both positive and negative, are credible. The best way to obtain this proof is by examination of the product, which is the output of the organization you are auditing.

In a factory, product is pretty easy to identify. Valves, canned peas, relays, tires, and doors can be seen. The product of a service group is harder to define. Try to come up with something tangible. For example, the product of a purchasing group might be the finished purchase order. The product of a human resources group might be an offer of employment and subsequent employment contract. The product of a government agency might be a regulatory decision. The product of a call center could be an accurate order. Regardless of the activity being audited, you must find a way to tie your conclusions back to something tangible. The easiest way to accomplish this connection is through the technique of tracing.

TRACING

Tracing is a common means of collecting objective evidence (facts) during an audit. It can involve almost every facet of the system being examined and will result in a well-defined picture of actual practices. To trace means to follow the progress of something as it is processed (see Figure 4.2). The item being traced may be tangible, such as a milk bottle, or intangible, such as information. The way to start is to pull out the flowchart of the activity, which you prepared in step six of the preparation phase. This can be used as a road map for your tracing.

The mechanics of tracing are relatively simple:

- Start either at the beginning, middle, or the end of the process.
- Choose an action, such as painting a wall.
- Gather information on the six process forces (methods, machinery, material, manpower, measurement, and environment) for that action. Be sure to record this information on your checklist. Write

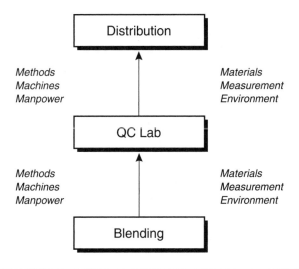

Figure 4.2 Tracing the activity.

down what you see, the person you are talking to, where you are, when the action was done, why the action is accomplished, and how it is accomplished. These become your facts for later use.
- Follow the path of the transaction backward or forward through the process.

It is usually more meaningful to trace a product backward through the process. Start with distribution, then proceed to the lab, then go to final blending, then go to solvent extraction, and so on. A note of caution is needed here. The auditee may not understand why you want to go against the normal flow of activities. Be patient. By tracing backward, you are examining product actually being produced or shipped. This stuff is going to the internal and external customer. Your conclusions will represent reality, not some "what if" situation.

When performing a supplier audit, a slight modification might be of value. Before you leave, make a copy of a recent purchase order to the supplier. After you arrive on site, look at the order entry process to see how your requirements were analyzed and put into the production stream. Then look at production planning to see how the various work instructions were developed for your order. Traveler sheets, inspection plans, and Bill of Material forms are possible documents that will be used for your work. You have covered the front-end planning. Now go to the back-end activities, such as packaging and shipping, to examine recent shipments. Continue tracing backward until you get to production planning.

Data collection by tracing rests upon the assumption that the path taken fairly represents the actual functioning of the process. Therefore, you must be careful while being led through the maze by your guide. Match what you are seeing with what you studied in the preparation phase. If significant differences arise, ask why.

INTERVIEWS

This is the process of obtaining information from another person in response to your questions. It is the most important form of data you can gather in auditing. It is also very difficult to do. At first you will be very nervous. This is not something most folks come by naturally. It has to be practiced.

Although considerable information is obtained through an interview, it cannot usually be regarded as conclusive because of communication barriers we erect between one another. This is done for survival and protection against harm. As humans, we put invisible barriers up to define our private space. The studies generally put our personal space as a circle about three feet in radius. (Perhaps that is because you can hit someone within the length of your arm!) As auditors, you are entering their space. Discomfort with your presence increases as you get closer. You may not have heard the reply; they may not have heard the question. Additionally, the other party may not have the big picture as you do. When someone tells you something, it is not yet a fact. It is a pseudo-fact. Only after that statement has been corroborated can you say for sure that you have a fact.

There are three ways to corroborate the information received in an interview:

1. Another person says the same thing. Of course, they need not use the exact same words, but the message (information) is the same as that heard earlier. To have maximum value, try to choose someone from another group or management level to corroborate the first story.
2. Another member of your team hears the same thing. The information can come from the same person you spoke with earlier or another person. Regardless of the second source, another set of ears has received the same message, so the likelihood of a miscommunication is less.
3. An item, document, or record verifies the action. You've heard the explanation and then read a procedure stating the action as explained. Or perhaps you see a completed form with the information just described.

None of these methods will show that the action is correct, but they will allow you to place faith in the information just received. The methods described may be right or they may not be right, but they are now fact. If you get stories that conflict, you do not have a fact. If you get 10 different versions of an action from 12 people, the fact is, "Nobody knows the correct method." You must get enough sources saying the same thing to allow you to state, "Yup. I now know the truth."

INTERVIEW TECHNIQUE

A good auditor possesses skill, training, and personal attitudes of a special nature. Part of this magical quality is the ability to conduct useful interviews. (Recall from earlier discussion that an interview is one of the five forms of data and that data are required in order to write a report.)

The interview process can be broken down into six steps.[1]

1. Put the person at ease.
2. Explain your purpose.

3. Find out what they are doing.
4. Analyze what they are doing.
5. Make a tentative conclusion.
6. Explain your next step.

In each of these steps, you must deal with the human person. Remember that they possess the information you need for success!

Put Them at Ease

Consider yourself as a guest in their home and show the respect you would naturally give to your host. Your purpose here is to give that other person an opportunity to size you up and to lower the natural sense of anxiety. This step may range from a simple introduction and handshake to discussions about the parking lot or weather. Often, the person being interviewed is threatened by your presence and may even perceive their job to be in jeopardy if wrong answers are given. Unless these barriers are removed, little information will be obtained. A good opening might be, "What is your job and how long have you worked in this area?" The answers are easy and the person feels more comfortable. The introduction period should last about a minute.

Explain Your Purpose

The natural first reaction to your presence might be, "Why me?" You must address that concern immediately. What information do you want? Why are you asking all these questions? Most people will express a desire to share information once they know why you want it. In this way it makes them feel important. A useful technique here is to show the other person a copy of your blank checklist. Right away, they can see the questions, understand the data you need, and make a decision as to whether they have that information. Of course, ask for your checklist back at the end of the discussion, so that you may use it again.

Demonstration of competence is important in this early stage of the interview process. You should be aware of the effect your appearance has on others and dress in a smart, businesslike manner. The impression you create by being well-organized and exhibiting knowledge of the subject matter is important. You need not be an expert in the processes, but you should at least be aware of the commonly used terms and associated methods. Use words they understand, without talking up or down to them. Be careful, however, to refrain from discussing explicit controls or practices that you have seen elsewhere. Such showing off will only damage your usefulness. Of course, you should never discuss business-sensitive matters with unauthorized people.

Find Out What They Are Doing

During your preparation for the audit, you should have examined the various documents affecting this area. You have already identified areas to explore. You now continue the investigation process by asking open-ended questions: "How does the Ogden Service Center use this information?" "What is your first action upon receipt of a data input form?" "What are the common actions or events that start this program going?" Use questions that begin with who, what, where, when, why, and how.[2] By avoiding questions which give yes or no answers, you will get much more information. If the answers are incomplete, try, "And then what happens?"

Prior to your audit, nearly everyone was told, "Just answer the question! Do not embellish." The questions you ask here are not the same as those that appear on your checklist. These are the mental guides designed to get you the data. One open-ended question will probably get you several answers for your checklist.

You should also avoid statements such as "I understand you keep the Tool Inventory Sheet." In legal circles this is called a leading question and is designed to elicit a specific response. The way you phrase the question leads the respondent to give you the answer they think you are expecting.

During this part of the interview process, it is necessary to get that other person to show you the forms, printouts, flow meters, Web pages, and drill bits being discussed. Get as close to the operations as you safely can, with minimal disruption of the work. Remember that you need facts for your conclusions. This not only helps you to understand the control process, it also contributes to the examination by providing concrete examples of the verbal explanations.

It also directs some of the natural tension toward an inanimate object. You do not audit in a conference room. You audit in the workspaces.

You have two ears and one mouth, so you should probably listen twice as long as you talk! This is certainly not the time to lecture the other person or brag about your accomplishments. If your question produces a satisfactory answer, make a notation on your checklist and proceed to the next question. The necessary pause periods while you write should be as brief as possible. You should always strive to reduce tensions; silence is usually uncomfortable. One technique that is often quite effective is to write out loud as you place information on your checklist.

Also remember that this is not a trial. Avoid using small voice recorders. They only intimidate and allow you to become lazy.

You now have a bunch of marks and notes on your checklist. You have gathered a lot of information, but you are not finished with the interview yet! Some important (and often forgotten) steps follow.

Analyze What They Are Doing

Once you have heard the words, you must analyze what those words mean. If you are familiar with the process being discussed, your job here becomes somewhat easier. When there is a logical break in the questioning, repeat the answers back, using different words, to improve the chance that you understand. "Let me see if I have that straight. First you receive the item and note its properties and then you attach the screws." Such thinking out loud, also known as paraphrasing, forces you to put the facts in perspective and in some sort of logical arrangement. Draw boxes and flowcharts on your checklist notes. Underline important issues. Draw stars.

Sometimes you will receive an answer that is incomplete or clearly at variance with the written requirements. Attempt to resolve the issue by looking for areas of agreement and defer the area of disagreement for later. Give the other person the opportunity to save face. The omission or lack of control may not have been important after all, or it may have been an inadvertent error. It is useful to stress supporting or contributing statements. Try to stay away from the insignificant.

This step is one of the most difficult for those just learning to audit. Not only do you have to actively listen to the words, but you also have to match the incoming data with your understanding of the requirements. At the same time, you are writing notes on your checklist and developing words for the next question. It's hard!

Make a Tentative Conclusion

It is now time to state your conclusions. This concept of *no secrets* is sometimes hard to practice; we don't want to tell someone that they are doing something wrong. This is why annual performance reports are often deferred or meaningless. But you are obligated to tell the interviewee what you think. Your final report will benefit as well.

If your initial analysis indicates that all is well, it is appropriate to say, "I see you are checking the finished surface every 45 minutes and that meets the requirements of APC 27." Let that other person know that he or she is doing something good. They will continue to perform well with such recognition by an outsider.

If there is a deficiency, give them an opportunity to produce additional factual evidence to show that you have made an error. The discussion should be unemotional and professional. Do not convey glee at having found a deficiency or anger at what seems to be an evasive answer. Remember that you will have the last word in the report. You know it and they know it. Taking a stand or playing win/lose rarely solves problems. If doubt remains at the end of the discussion, then say so. Do not say, "You haven't convinced me that your actions are correct." Rather say, "There still seems to be an opening here. Perhaps I'll understand it better when I review more data."

By practicing this philosophy of "no secrets," any errors you may have made will be corrected early in this interview phase rather than at a formal closing meeting or after the report is issued. There is a strong desire on the part of that other person to make your problem disappear. Turn that tentative conclusion around. To do so, the person must give you additional facts and provide you with more data. You have just turned that other person into an auditor! You have, in effect, leveraged your audit. If their argument is successful and your problem is resolved, that other person wins. (Yes, you want to encourage disagreements while they are small and easier to resolve.) If their argument is unsuccessful, eventually that other person will be convinced that a problem exists. The auditor wins again, in that the problem can now be corrected. Additionally, you have provided vital feedback to the employee; good performance will continue and poor performance will be corrected. Everyone wins!

The principle of "no secrets" means you leave the door open for resolution. You do not take a stand. You do not wait until you have a tight case with convincing facts. You do not say, "You fool! You have a finding!" Rather, you say, "I think there is a problem here. It looks like you have no way to check the blade sharpness before you use it."

Explain Your Next Step

The final step of the interview process is to conclude the discussions and let that other person know what's next. If you feel that you have about all the information you can get, then state, "Thank you for your help. I don't believe we'll need to get back with you again." Whew! The person can now go back to work and once more be a productive employee. If all your questions have not been answered, you may wish to make another appointment. If you intend to check out additional records as a result of the interview, then this, too, should be stated. It is important to remember that people want to know the following:

- How they did in the interview
- Whether they are finished

The keys to a good interview are rigorous preparation, and a genuine desire to know and understand the other person's viewpoint. You must remember that these are other human beings and not printed circuit boards. They have the advantage of having a valuable commodity (information) that you desire. If you act like a guest in their home and stick to the principle of *no secrets,* your interview will be a success.

PERCEPTIONS

Most of us recognize that the world as we see it is not necessarily as it really is. A good job to one of us may be a sloppy job to another. Often, we are presented with the same set of facts as someone else. Our perception of these facts and resulting conclusions will be different depending upon our individual needs and viewpoints (as shown in Figure 4.3). People, including auditors, see things differently. You may have developed considerable bias over time. You may have familiarity with the company way of doing things. Of course, the same thing has happened to those you will be auditing. These different views may be quite honestly and stubbornly held.

You must recognize this situation and attempt to overcome it. Here are some concepts to consider if you wish to persuade your customers that your perception of the facts is better (more useful) than their perception of those same facts:

- Present items and facts that will satisfy the needs of the affected organizations. You should make a contribution by showing how the facts affect the product or service.

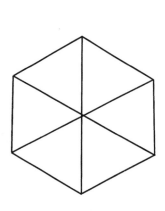

Figure 4.3 Two common illustrations of differing perceptions.[3]

- Ignore or downplay mildly disturbing things. Strive to answer the "So what?" reaction.
- Pay attention to significant things. Chronic or persistent problems and weaknesses, along with trends, will get the attention of your audience.
- Above all, try to focus on business values. We all listen to radio station WII-FM (What's in it for Me). Songs heard over WII-FM include cost, schedule, grievances, overtime, customer complaints, and missed shipments. These are the important driving forces in the lives of your intended audience.

Granted, these concepts have much to do with the report of the audit and the way in which you present your conclusions, but you must be aware of these needs and perceptions during the performance phase in order to gather the proper information. Additionally, you will have many opportunities to present small summaries and conclusions throughout the audit. You should be prepared to address these perception issues from the beginning.

TEAM MEETINGS

You should make time prior to lunch and at the end of each day for your team to meet. Thirty minutes for each of these meetings should be enough. These caucus sessions should be informal discussions amongst only the audit team members. Ask your guide to take a break. You accomplish three things during these short team meetings:

1. Share facts, concerns, and problems.
2. Adjust your data-gathering activities. This is sort of a repeat of the preparation phase.
3. Develop the report by proposing possible conclusions.

Sharing facts and tentative conclusions enriches the audit process. Talking over what has been learned during the day's investigation allows for team corroboration of facts and possible areas for deeper investigation. Discussions should also include the perceptions drawn during the interview process. Is there an activity that is done extremely well or very poorly? Do the facts gathered by each individual team member point to a more general conclusion about the controls used and their implementation? The questions and discussions should bring into sharper focus tentative conclusions for the report. Facts collected during the day should be organized and sorted in order to support these conclusions, both positive and negative. Where pieces of evidence are either insufficient or completely missing, you can then make plans to fill in these gaps.

The result from this sharing could be redirection of the audit. Keep in mind, however, that you are obligated to stick to the original purpose and scope. Based on information now available, the following issues can be addressed:

- Are the results of the interviews and other data gathering sufficient to reach a conclusion?
- Should there be additional interviews, additional checklist questions, or additional records reviewed? Do you need more data?
- Are there administrative problems to be resolved with the group being audited or your audit team?
- Does the audit seem to be accomplishing its objectives?

As you conduct interviews and gather data, you will reach conclusions about the performance of the auditee. You should write these down in draft form. They may be either good or bad practices, but they should be considered for the final report. At the team meeting these draft statements may be polished, consolidated with others, or discarded. In any event they are extremely useful for beginning the reporting phase.

DAILY BRIEFINGS

You can see that effective team meetings are important to success. Likewise, daily briefings with the auditee will enhance the quality of your audit. If a goal of improved performance is to be attained, it is important that there be no surprises at all levels. This communication can be strengthened by a short and informal briefing of about 10 minutes at the end of each day with a representative from the group, normally your guide or shadow. Topics to be discussed include:

- Checklist areas completed
- Checklist areas to be examined (or revisited) tomorrow
- Any areas of concern
- Any problems experienced

If you've uncovered something out of whack, it is certainly not necessary (or desirable) to present polished conclusions yet. Rather, explain to the representative that these are potential problem areas or areas of concern at this stage. You know that as soon as this meeting is finished, the representative will brief his or her manager. They will all try to make your problem go away. The auditee organization becomes motivated to help you by providing additional facts to verify or refute your concerns. If you were wrong because of incorrect or insufficient information, the item is prevented from appearing in the final report. If they truly do have a problem, the additional investigating has helped to reinforce the fact. Either way, both parties win.

ONWARD

The next phase of the audit process is the reporting phase, although you may have noticed that much of the discussion in this chapter has concerned itself with the report. This is because there is no sharp boundary line between data gathering and reporting. The report is being proposed, modified, rejected, and rebuilt by the entire team both individually and jointly as the audit progresses. You must keep it in the back of your mind constantly. Starting the report on the first day of data gathering has at least four merits:

1. It helps structure the audit by forcing you to develop hypotheses early.
2. The writing of tentative conclusions forces precision in the process.
3. The problem of sorting, understanding, and reviewing a large mass of material before the exit meeting deadline is reduced.
4. Factual errors, perceptual errors, and other distortions are reduced.

The next chapter contains more detailed discussion on the specific aspects of your report.

ENDNOTES

1. Original concept developed by Frank X. Brown, *The Practice and Process of Auditing* (Pittsburgh: Westinghouse Electric Corporation, 1979).
2. "I keep six honest serving men (They taught me all I knew); Their names are What and Why and When and How and Where and Who." From Rudyard Kipling, "The Elephant Child," in *Just-So Stories* (New York: Knopf, 1992).
3. The figure on the left could be a three-dimensional cube, or it could be a six-sided flat hexagon. The figure on the right could be an old or young woman. Some even see an eagle and a sea otter!

THE REPORT IS YOUR PRODUCT

The audit report is your final product. All of the sights, sounds, smells, observations, scraps of paper, tensions, and anxieties are finally reduced into something for others to read. When everything is closed out, the only evidence of your presence is the report! It is your means of communicating information to others. As such, it should have certain characteristics in order to be successful.

REPORT CHARACTERISTICS

Reports should have accuracy, conciseness, clarity, timeliness, and tone.[1] The report must be completely factual, in that every statement and reference must be based on one of the five forms of data discussed in the preceding chapter. It must be concise so that superfluous words do not block reception of the message. A clear report puts your thoughts into the mind of the reader. Timely reports examine topics while they are of interest. Results are published before they are forgotten. Finally, the tone of the report must be courteous and professional. It must sound like the voice of management.

In addition to these traits, which are common to all reports, your report needs to possess the additional characteristics of relevance, consistency, and comparability.[2] Unless your report is relevant to the business needs of your customers, it will be largely ignored. Consistency of reports over time will show trends and provide for greater comprehension by the reader. After they are familiar with format and contents, they know where to look for desired information. Finally, reports from a number of auditors should be comparable to allow for maximum efficiency and fairness.

Your reports should be verifiable. The reader may not always be able to personally verify them, since we cannot track down the evidence for every piece of history known. But if you use generally accepted names for things (for example, foot, yard, milling machine, and batch preparation files), there is less danger of your message being misunderstood. When you refer to specific items or locations at the audit site (but not individual names!), the perception of verifiability is enhanced. Of course, one of the main purposes of a structured checklist is to record supporting information (facts). However, putting checklist-like detail in the report makes it too cumbersome and unreadable. Additionally, the reader tends to become tangled in the checklist details and may miss the overall message of the report. Your completed checklists should be kept in the office file as background data. These are field notes and should not be included with the report.

DESIRE TO TRUST

Even though it appears (especially to the new auditor) as if everybody seems to be quarreling with everybody else, we still trust information from others. We ask street directions of total strangers. We follow directions on microwave popcorn packages without being suspicious of the people who wrote those directions. We read books about science, space travel, the history of party dresses, and even fishing, and we assume that the author is trying hard to tell the true story. Most of the time, we are safe in our assumptions. There is an enormous amount of reliable information available. Deliberate misinformation is still more the exception than the rule. The reader wants to believe your report because of basic human desires. With simple, clear, and direct language, you can reinforce those desires.

INFERENCES

An inference is a statement about the unknown made on the basis of the known. You may infer lack of process control over donut size from your initial knowledge of donut production and your subsequent examination of the blending and mixing instructions. You may infer lack of actual control from the fact that six out of 24 donuts pulled from the line were too small. An audit requires that you make such inferences. The question is not, "Should you make inferences?" but rather, "Are you aware of the inferences you make?" The technique of gathering and analyzing facts will allow you to present these inferences in an understandable and logical fashion. Anyone may retrace your path and should make the same inference. But since this is unlikely to happen, you must take the approach that a reasonable person, presented with the same facts you have seen, will draw conclusions similar to yours. Their inferences will match yours.

As a practical matter, most people will need more convincing (stronger facts and more of them) if the inference does not support a previously held conviction. This is not surprising. Any student of debate knows that it is quite difficult to change a long-held perception, even if that perception is wrong.

JUDGMENTS

Judgments are expressions of approval or disapproval. Like inferences, they are part of your report. As with inferences, those judgments supporting a previously held belief will be accepted quickly. Judgments contrary to those beliefs will be resisted. If your judgments are of an adverse nature, they may be subject to distortion on the receiving end unless you take great pains to make them as clear and understandable as possible.

PAIN AND PLEASURE

As humans, we respond to two basic forces—pain and pleasure. If you show people that their actions are causing them to experience pain, they will do everything in their power to remove that pain. Likewise, show that their actions are causing pleasure and they will continue those actions. That's the way we are. As an auditor, you must show the pain resulting from nonconforming conditions.

Your customers are usually those in charge of the area being audited. You must show the pain in terms they can understand. This means you must find the adverse business conditions. Scrap, rework, missed deliveries, cut fingers, overtime, regulatory fines, and miscommunications are all examples of pain. Through the data-gathering phase, you have gathered a number of facts. The closer you can tie those facts to the goods and services being produced, the more successful you will be in convincing others that their actions are causing pain (or pleasure).

FINDINGS

As we saw in the earlier chapters, a *finding* comes from analyzing the raw data (facts) of an audit. Many audit programs use the term *finding* for only unsatisfactory conclusions of an audit. The conformity assessment program, involving third-party registration, tends to use the term *nonconformity*. Because of this diversity in use, it has been difficult to define these terms in the published audit program standards around the word.[3] Often, the term *finding* has a different meaning from one company or agency to another. In general, however, it means something bad. Seldom is a *finding* presented as a positive (or neutral) conclusion.

A finding is an audit conclusion that identifies a condition having a significant adverse effect on the quality of the activity under review. A finding has the following characteristics:

- It is negative. Something is amiss.
- It is a violation of a requirement. A promise was made and it was not kept.
- It is significant. It is a big deal. It relates to business values and is affecting those values in an adverse manner.

Other terms may be used for audit conclusions in your organization. Some of these other terms are concern, major or minor nonconformity, and deficiency. (We discussed misuse of the term *observation* earlier in the preparation phase.) The words are used in many different ways, so you need to take steps to assure that the reader knows their meaning. First, you should define each term in your local audit procedure. That way, you and other auditors in your group will be speaking the same language. Second, define the terms in your report. Do this by placing the definition in parentheses immediately after the first appearance of that word. That way, the reader will know exactly what you mean. See Appendix B for a list of common audit terms.

PREPARING THE FINDING SHEETS

Before your exit meeting (discussed later in this chapter), you need to assemble your team for one more long, and serious, meeting. This last meeting takes about twice as long as the previous ones. Your goal is to develop the finding statements (if things are amiss) or positive practice statements (if things are swell) or both. Of course, if you don't have any findings or positive practices, you can go right into developing the overall summary.

First, collect and discuss all of the good and bad facts uncovered during the course of the audit. All the team members should review their individual field notes. The audit team leader acts as scribe, to make a master list of these good and bad facts. Don't attempt to figure out the causes and patterns yet; just write down all of the good and bad facts.

Take your list of bad facts and start analyzing and sorting the data by problem. State the problem and put all the facts associated with that problem on the pile. Do the same for the other problems. If a bad fact applies to several problems, replicate it and place it on both piles. This is classic data chunking or sorting.

An amazing thing happens. You will always have one or two piles that are bigger than the rest. Focus on these big piles. Set aside the problems with only one or two bad facts. These are minor issues and we will deal with them later.

Cause and Effect

Look at each of the big piles, one at a time. What is the pain? How is this adversely affecting the business, the risks, the internal efficiencies, and so on? At this point you are starting to become subjective. That's OK, as long as the statements clearly show some pain within the area being audited. As humans, we basically react to two forces—pain and pleasure. If you show a person that their actions are causing pain, there is a desire to make the pain go away. Showing a person that their actions are causing pleasure will cause a desire to continue or increase that pleasure. Pain and pleasure are basic human drivers!

As auditors, you must show *business pain*. This means scrap, rework, overtime, missed delivery, lost sales, or regulatory fines. We must go back to the three universal business forces of cost, production, and risk. This is pain.

After you have identified the pain, write down the cause of that pain. Look at your list of adverse facts. Try to see the patterns and connections. Go back to the external policy documents and internal system descriptions to determine the larger areas of weakness. Remember the fishbone diagram and other statistical process control tools.[4]

Each finding must be a clear, concise statement of a generic problem, one that relates to a whole group, class, or activity. A single nonconformance, such as, "Printing software, being used for the generation of Starbird program reports, was not the current version," is not a finding. In this case the corrective action taken by the office will probably be limited to replacing that software module with the current version. No attempt will be made to find out why the obsolete version was being used in that group. Certainly, no effort will be taken to try to implement a software module control procedure, train personnel, or take other steps to address the underlying cause of this specific problem.

If there are a number of examples of incorrect versions in use, there is indeed a generic problem. But you still don't have a very strong case and haven't convinced management that a true problem exists. You need to show how similar problems fit into the picture. For example, a construction audit team might have gathered the following facts:

1. Out-of-date blueprints were being used at seven of nine milepost work areas.
2. The blueprint control register was last revised on March 6th, which is three months past the date required by Engineering Procedure 7.5.
3. Redlined drawings were noted in the guardrail fabrication shop, without evidence of approval authority. This is in violation of Engineering Procedure 3.6.
4. Twelve percent of the guardrails between mileposts 287 and 289 required rework.
5. Field inspection change notices were not referenced on 12 blueprints in use, as required by Construction Order 6-2.
6. Contractor rework of signal controls, costing $80,000, was due to the use of an incorrect specification.

All of these should be consolidated into one truly generic finding, such as: "Work instruction documents are not effectively controlled. This is causing cost overruns and schedule delays."

Now list the individual facts that show the basis for your statement. Each of these bad facts should be numbered so that they may stand-alone. It is not necessary to place the supporting bad facts in any particular order, other than logical. They should flow. The facts logically lead to the finding. A reasonable person (the reader) seeing those facts will draw the same conclusion that you have drawn.

The finding has two elements: cause and effect. The cause is the problem statement. The effect is business pain. When you list your facts beneath this finding, you now have a *finding sheet* (see Figure 5.1).

Statement of the Problem

A variation on the above approach is to just state the problem, rather than full cause and effect. You would still list the supporting bad facts under the problem statement (see Figure 5.2). This presentation is generally

AUDIT FINDING	Audit No.: 03-32 Audit Date: November 10–12, 2003 Team Leader: Sarah Margaret Sears
Problem Statement:	Inadequate equipment maintenance is causing customer dissatisfaction and reduced business.
Supporting Facts:	1. During the Monday morning peak rush period, 10 customers requested clean plates after receiving breakfast orders. 2. The water filter on the automatic dish-washer has not been cleaned or changed since October of 2001. City Health Department code specifies twice a year. 3. Twice during the Monday lunch period, the coffee machine overflowed. The manufacturer's instructions recommend daily cleaning. The coffee unit is not listed in the cleaning schedule. 4. The number of customer comment cards has doubled within the last six months. 5. Customers tend to avoid the tables on the south side. These are the most difficult tables to service. 6. Cooks are unable to control oven temperatures within 50 degrees. 7. Two of 20 counter stools are no longer safe to sit on and have been removed from service.

Figure 5.1 Finding sheet with cause and effect.

better for compliance audits, where affected managers and supervisors all agree that the audit criteria are correct. In theory, they do not need convincing. In reality, there are probably some doubts. Logical arrangement of the bad facts under the problem will reduce those doubts.

The smaller process and product audits will also use this method to show results.

AUDIT FINDING	Audit No.: 03-32 Audit Date: November 10–12, 2003 Team Leader: Sarah Margaret Sears
Problem Statement:	Fixtures and equipment are not maintained in accordance with requirements.
Supporting Facts:	1. During the Monday morning peak rush period, 10 customers requested clean plates after receiving breakfast orders. 2. Of the 50 plates ready for use at 8 A.M. on Tuesday, 15 had food particles on them. 3. The water filter on the automatic dishwasher has not been cleaned or changed since October of 2001. City Health Department code specifies twice a year. 4. Twice during the Monday lunch period, the coffee machine overflowed. The manufacturer's instructions recommend daily cleaning. The coffee unit is not listed in the cleaning schedule. 5. Cooks are unable to control oven temperatures within 50 degrees. 6. Two of 20 counter stools are no longer safe to sit on and have been removed from service.

Figure 5.2 Finding sheet with problem statement.

Judgment Is Required

A finding is a subjective opinion (judgment) supported by fact. Each of the facts, by themselves, may or may not be important. When they are combined, however, the reader can see the system failure. Findings are the disease; facts are the symptoms of that disease. This is the main difference between an audit and an inspection. Inspectors report problems. Auditors must analyze events for reasons. They show the management issues in need of correction. Inspection is part of the auditing process, but auditing is far more than inspection. Inspectors report nonconformance. Auditors tell us why those nonconforming events happened.

In order to serve our customers, we must show that the control systems either work or they do not work. Managers are looking for assurances that they are performing the tasks of planning, directing, and controlling in an effective fashion.

RECOMMENDATIONS

Prior to the 1990s, it was common to see the auditors placing recommendations in their reports. When the first edition of this book came out in 1987, I suggested that the practice could actually be harmful. Many of my colleagues thought otherwise. Today, it is the opposite. The practice of placing recommendations in the report has fallen out of favor. As seen above, there are better ways to achieve improved performance.

When the audit group starts to provide solutions to another organization's problems, the inevitable result is a decrease in the quality of the product or service. There are several reasons for this.

Malicious Compliance

The receiving organization often does not know what you really mean in a suggestion and may be angry with you for making it in the first place. So they do an obviously stupid thing just to show you how far off base you are. Remember that the quickest way to get your boss in trouble is to do exactly what he or she says. Then you can always say, "I did just what you told me to do."

Inadequate Knowledge

Problems by their very nature are often difficult to solve. At times, this may require a very extensive analysis or an in-depth investigation. In the limited time for an audit, the team cannot always devote the resources necessary to find the true underlying cause(s) to a difficult problem, so the solution is inadequate. Don't be tempted to suggest some meaningless approaches for solving the problem, when you don't have enough information.

Perceived Bias

You may be tempted to suggest or recommend a solution based upon your prior experience in a similar situation. But because your solution was *not invented here* (NIH), it becomes suspect and you stand a chance of being accused of bias.

Ownership of Quality

If you allow yourself to recommend, suggest, or direct the necessary corrective action, then you have assumed at least partial ownership of the problem, with little or no resources to correct it. This is not an ideal position to be in. You have become a consultant to the organization on the receiving end of the recommendation. Ownership of the quality of the product or service is no longer clearly defined; you have taken some of that ownership away. And when you take away ownership, you remove responsibility and accountability.

This concept of the ownership of quality is most important to success. Managers and supervisors are paid good money to provide quality products and services and must be held accountable for the resulting work. The job of an auditor is to provide analyzed information, as another set of eyes and ears for the various stakeholders. You must find and analyze the true impediments to quality and then let affected managers and supervisors correct those problems.

No Longer Necessary

Recommendations were necessary when only symptoms were reported. To make up for the lack of analysis, auditors presented specific recommended solutions. They rarely worked. The auditor would return and see the same problem. Frustration was common.

If you report your results as a statement of the problem, followed by facts, the recommendation becomes obvious. Fix the problem.

PRESENTING YOUR INFORMATION

Does this mean that the auditors should just point out problems and then walk away? Of course you should not. But you must not impose your methods and approaches on the audited group. If asked during the audit, then offer the benefit of your experience in having seen good and not-so-good methods. Offer to put the auditee in contact with others who have had the same problem. Give them a copy of the recent magazine article about it. When working with a supplier, be careful not to give away competitive information of trade secrets in your desire to assist.

As we transition from compliance to performance auditing, this becomes a difficult issue. Your desire is to add value by offering sound advice. You have studied all the external and internal requirements. You have analyzed the data for effectiveness and suitability. You have seen more of the firm than perhaps anyone else. You want to be able to do something with all that knowledge and vision.

On the other hand, you do not have all the answers. Nor are you privy to many of the internal and external forces driving the organization, such as distribution problems in Malaysia, impending retirement of Dorothy, or the current negotiations for a major equipment upgrade. You really should leave the supervising to the supervisors.

As you struggle with these two opposing desires, try to phrase your oral and written words such that meaningful direction is provided without specific detail. In reality, your advice may not be seen as optional for the auditee. There is a great deal of pressure to do precisely what the auditor says, whether it contributes to quality or makes things worse. Some of your managers have a strong desire to keep a low profile. Those who rock the boat may not be seen as team players. Their careers could suffer. You should be aware of this reaction in your discussions with the auditee. Carefully phrase your conversations as solicited advice rather than required actions. Even though the report has yet to be issued, some of your utterances may become edict.

Remember that a finding is a condition adverse to quality. If not corrected, the quality of the group being evaluated will continue to suffer. Remember, too, that the main objective of an audit is to improve the performance of the area or activity being examined. This requires that findings be stated in terms that will arouse management interest and convince them that there are serious problems that must be investigated and corrected. Even though you have not made a direct recommendation for the fix, you have accomplished the same thing. The reader will see your words and want to change, because you have shown them (through the use of facts) the pain. However, they own that decision and its subsequent action.

SIX OR LESS

Your audit reports should usually contain six or fewer findings. We know that a small percentage of certain characteristics will account for a high percentage of resulting problems. The importance of distinguishing the vital few from the trivial many[5] can be seen in almost any situation. For audits, this means that the vital few problems will make the major contribution to the lack of quality in most organizations.

Our poor little brains tend to overload when presented with too many problems simultaneously. As a result, none get the attention they truly deserve. Your readers can effectively address and resolve five problems; they cannot address 50.

If you discover that you continually report a large number of so-called findings, you are still listing symptoms. You have not done the analysis to determine the common control issues. You need to group more things together. You need to dig deeper. You need to analyze the situation further, to determine the system failures causing all of these discrepant items.

OVERALL CONCLUSIONS

Next, you need to develop an overall summary statement of everything you have examined. This is the bottom line. It includes the good as well as the bad. The credibility and acceptance of your message (and your written report) is substantially improved when it includes an evaluation of overall performance. "How well are we doing?" is a fair question. For supplier audits, you are thinking (but not writing), "Should we give them additional business?" Of course, only the purchasing group can change supplier direction, but you have helped them to provide that direction. Is the operation safe? Are there satisfactory resources to accomplish the tasks? Some statement of analysis will go a long way in meeting the needs of your audit boss. Remember that you're getting paid to answer the two basic questions of whether the control systems are in place and if they work. The summary is, therefore, the most important part of your entire report. Despite opinions to the contrary, it's OK to state that things are working well, like they should be, and that only a few minor problems exist.

Usually, a one-paragraph general discussion of the overall program controls is sufficient. Because most of your readers are managers and supervisors, the words should be phrased in management terms. An example for an audit of the training program is:

> The training program is being effectively implemented. Training needs have been defined. Adequate resources exist to provide identified training. Knowledge is demonstrated on the line and in the shops. However, in the area of steam valve maintenance, some newly hired technicians were unsure of the proper stem lubricant to use.

Such a statement gives management a feeling of security in their implementation of this area. It also allows them to focus on the one remaining issue.

EXIT MEETING

The exit meeting is the first formal opportunity for you to present your report to the group managers. Typically, the data-gathering part of the audit is concluded some time on the morning of the final day. The exit interview is then scheduled for some time in the afternoon, and you are left with about two to four hours to prepare something for the exit interview. If you have practiced the principles of no secrets, daily team meetings, and keeping folks apprised of your progress and any concerns, then two hours is sufficient time to draft those findings, positive practices, and the summary.

Attendance

You should present your results to the responsible managers of the group you just audited. Several layers of management will most probably lead to argument. It is human nature to want to defend one's position in front of the boss, even if we know that position to be wrong. So a supervisor is obligated to argue a finding in his or her area if the director is present. Also, if all the managers are at your meeting, they are probably away from more productive work. You can limit this arguing and unproductive time by requesting attendance by only a few.

Conducting the Meeting

The exit meeting is the job of the team leader. It's tough and demanding, but that's your job. Above all, avoid any arguing among the team members during the exit meeting. The team speaks with one voice, that of the team leader's.

As the team leader, you should start with a statement that the audit is finished. You then say the courtesy things, such as your appreciation for the hospitality extended to you and your team. State that you have accomplished your task. After this introduction, you want to accomplish four things:

1. Present the summary.
2. Summarize any findings and positive practices.
3. Ask for any corrections or explanations of fuzzy areas.
4. Discuss the corrective action follow-up process (if problems were identified).

Give a short recap of the audit scope and purpose and then get right into the summary. The best way to do this is in the form of a personal conversation between you, representing the team, and the senior auditee manager present. Rather than read from a script, look at the people as you present the overall conclusions. Make them all feel that the subject matter is important and they are important as well. You should then present the highlights of any findings or positive practices. Don't go into great detail. Present the issues and praises in a straightforward fashion, followed by the more significant facts. You should not have to present all of the individual items leading to your conclusion.

Draft Conclusions

Now pass out copies of the draft finding or positive practice sheets. These are handwritten or printed from your laptop and assembled one to a page. There are several good reasons for doing this:

- It forces you to prepare for the exit meeting.
- It allows you to gather any remaining facts before you leave the audit area. Once the exit meeting is over, your access to additional data is severely limited.
- It keeps you honest. Often, you will be subjected to intense pressure to change your final report. For various reasons, some will want you to go easy on the auditee. Others will want you to get tough. By issuing your conclusions (in draft) at the exit meeting, you have committed yourself. You cannot "un-ring" a bell. You are in a better position to resist the pressure to change what was said at the exit meeting.

These draft conclusions don't have to be perfect. Handwritten words on a lined tablet will do. Do not read the words out loud. Give people credit for being able to read on their own. Explain the items in a conversational manner as briefly as you can, but remember that their listening abilities are diminished as they read the paper in front of them.

In the early days of auditing, it was common to have the auditee sign the bottom of the finding sheets. This was to indicate that they understood the finding and the facts. In reality, it was perceived as a forced confession. Most auditors now find the practice undesirable.

In preparing for the exit meeting, you should keep in mind that the facts and conclusions reached at the exit meeting must not be changed in the final report. You need a clear understanding on both sides—you and them. If you have any concerns to raise, put them in your notes and discuss them in the exit meeting. Be sensitive to the clues given by the auditee at that meeting. They may not see your logic, yet they want to remain respectful. Encourage communication. Failure to do so, particularly if your facts are wrong, casts doubt on the entire audit effort.

Finish Promptly

In preparing for the exit meeting, it is worthwhile to put yourself in the readers' position and see things from their viewpoint. Remember that your objective is to change things for the better (or at least encourage the continuance of good practices). The art of the exit meeting lies in persuading the auditee (and your audit boss) that your conclusions represent the true state of things. If problems were uncovered, then the consequences are serious and something can and should be done about them. If your conclusions are faulty, this is the time for clarity. Once the report is published and distributed, your faulty logic takes on a life of its own and is very hard to correct. Encourage healthy discussion and understanding. It is a tough and demanding challenge for the team leader. Once finished, your whole team is physically, mentally, and emotionally exhausted. The team should promptly leave the area and disperse.

Process Audit Exit Meeting

The above discussion deals with the larger system audit. If you're doing a smaller process audit, you don't need to assemble a large group of people. When you are finished with the fieldwork, go to a quiet place. Assemble your thoughts and compose your findings and positive practices. Think about the conclusion statement. Then go to the shift supervisor's office. State that your audit is finished. Present your summary and highlight any positive or negative conclusions. Then indicate that your report will be published within a week and leave promptly.

FORMAL REPORT

The formal report is the final communication of your audit to all three customers (auditee, audit boss, organization). It must stand by itself without need for reference material. A reasonably knowledgeable layman should be able to understand it without asking a series of questions. It should be issued within a reasonable time period after the exit meeting. Remember, the longer the report is held up in review, the more its importance diminishes to the auditee. You should issue the formal report for a system audit within two weeks of the exit meeting. One week should be sufficient for the process audit. These guidelines should not be difficult, if you write your conclusions (and perhaps summary) in draft before the exit meeting occurs.

Your written report should contain two to four sections:

1. Introduction
2. Overall summary
3. Adverse conclusions (findings)
4. Noteworthy accomplishments (positive practices)

Attach your finding or positive practice sheets to the back, as attachments to your report. The first two items, introduction and overall summary, are required in every report, even for the smaller process audit. The last two items are optional, depending on the outcome.

Introduction

The report should begin with a short introduction. It tells the reader why the audit was performed (purpose), what was examined (scope), and who participated in the audit (auditors and auditees). Just lift the purpose statement from the previously issued audit plan. The scope should be brief, telling the reader what you looked at and the product of that activity. If this is a supplier audit, give the plant location, relative size, and general customer base. When stating who did the auditing, list the audit team by name and identify the team leader. However, when discussing the auditee, avoid using names. Otherwise, you are pointing fingers at specific individuals, should the results be less than outstanding. Rather, specify groups, activities, or locations. Doing so will lessen the adversarial nature of the audit process. The introduction paragraph should be about two inches long. See the example in Figure 5.3.

Overall Summary

The summary paragraph should come next. As stated earlier, this is the most important section of the report. It's the bottom-line information to your customers. Are necessary controls present? Are these controls implemented across all activities? Do they work? Is the group achieving those higher-level controls required for world-class quality? The summary section must answer these questions, but it must also be kept brief, clear, and concise if you are to retain your audience. See the example in Figure 5.4.

A summary will balance out the (by definition) negative tone of any findings. As humans, we respond much better to criticism when we are told that the overall program is working, but there are a few areas in need of correction. The team will be recognized as competent and unbiased if the summary presents a professional, honest, and straightforward picture.

On the other hand, serious problems need focused attention from the readers of your report. If a supplier's poor quality management is jeopardizing your firm or the area just examined is running on chaotic energy alone, the summary should be a direct and blunt call to arms. Others depend on you to see the things they don't.

Introduction

A routine supplier audit of Metal Products (MetPro) was performed at the facility in Carbondale, Illinois, on November 12–13, 2002. The audit examined metal finishing services provided by MetPro on pieces designated for railroad application, including cleaning, coating, painting, and polishing. The audit concentrated on quality system and equipment changes since the last audit in February of 2001.

MetPro performs both abrasive and solution cleaning of ferrous and aluminum surfaces. They also perform chromate and sulfate anodizing. There are four large painting booths and a large paint-curing oven. Operations are conducted in a climate-controlled industrial park facility. MetPro is a mature firm. They have been in this location for about 30 years. At the time of the audit, the work force was approximately 120 associates.

Linda Beamer (lead) and Tim Johnson conducted the audit. This was Linda's second visit to the facility.

Figure 5.3 Example introduction paragraph.

Summary

The MetPro facility is well lighted in both process and inspection areas. Technical process instructions are available and used by operators and technicians. The facility continues to receive about five audits a year from various customers; although the number may decrease once the Metal Finishers Association (MFA) accredits them. MetPro has a close working relationship with the railroad end users of the various parts we make. Standards and specifications are available on site and current.

Coating solutions are maintained and periodically tested. Paint material continues to be purchased only from approved sources and is kept in a controlled storage area. Shelf life, mixing, and reduction are controlled. All pieces are inspected for workmanship prior to shipping. Associated process and inspection records are maintained online, with paper copies available when necessary.

Within the scope of the audit, no adverse findings were detected.

Figure 5.4 Example summary paragraph.

Adverse Conclusions (Findings)

These are short, one- to two-sentence statements of each of the problem areas (findings), if there are any. When you have problems to report, this combination of summary and highlighted findings will get the attention of senior management. This includes all three of your customers. If well prepared, the capsule statements should stimulate interest in hearing about the details. They stimulate a desire to do something about any problems reported by the audit team.

Noteworthy Accomplishments (Positive Practices)

Sometimes, during the course of an audit, you will come across a group performing exceptionally well. Should this condition be reported? You bet it should! Don't, however, water down your report by calling everything exceptional. Remember that people and groups are expected to perform well. That's why we pay them a salary every month. However, you should acknowledge those program controls that are above and beyond the call of duty. Do this by devoting a separate paragraph to a description of the situation and how it affects the quality of the program under examination. Call this a positive practice and place it at the end of your report. Your readers leave smiling.

Attachments

Next come the details for each finding and positive practice. These are your *finding sheets* and *positive practice sheets.* Since you already passed these out in draft at the exit meeting, it's simply a matter of polishing up the words and making them look pretty. Present findings before positive practices and place the most important findings first. Your audience will devote the most attention to whatever you list first. Arranging your findings by manual chapter or regulatory clause will inhibit your communication efforts.

Even though you may have many examples (facts) to support a particular finding, present only a single page of material for each finding or positive practice. You are no longer performing inspections. You are auditing. Your job is not to present the foreman with a "punch list" of discrepancies to fix. Your job is to convince through the judicious use of facts. Much like a debate, a few logically arranged facts will go far. When you get to the bottom of the page, stop writing and go on to the next finding.

Report Size

As an auditor, your job is to communicate to management. Your customers are busy people. Everyone else is throwing information at them. What makes you so special that they should stop everything and read your report for the next two hours? Nothing. If you want your report to be read, keep the size to two pages, plus any findings or positive practices as attachments (see Figure 5.5). The process audit can be presented in one page plus attachments. Five pages will get read, but 50 pages will not reach your audience.

REPORT DISTRIBUTION

You should not send the report directly to the auditee. As an auditor, you work for the audit boss (see Figure 5.6). Send your report to your boss. This accomplishes three important objectives:

Figure 5.5 Audit report.

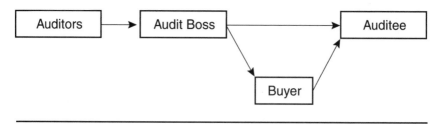

Figure 5.6 Releasing the report.

1. It forces the audit boss to read your report. Your boss has a better understanding of the issues and can better represent you and your audit group to others.
2. It promotes accountability of the audit function. By signing the cover letter, the issuing manager owns a portion of the report, even if you drafted the cover letter. This ownership encourages the boss to look for clarity and other communication issues. Fairness is promoted. The overall excellence of the audit group is higher. Good reports are encouraged and poor reports are rewritten.
3. If you have any findings, the auditee will be asked to provide an action plan for fixing the problems. You have no authority to request such a response. For supplier audits, this is a contractual matter and must be done by the buyer or purchasing agent.

This is not to imply that your audit boss must approve your team's audit report. This individual was not there and did not smell the roses; and, therefore, should not be asked to report on the aroma. The report is yours alone. However, your audit boss is responsible for the adequacy and quality of your product. This can be accomplished through the normal supervisory review process without compromising your independence and integrity.

Normally, you will send the report to the audit boss as an e-mail attachment. The audit boss will probably use most of your message body text to send the report on to others. If distribution is still by paper, you may be asked to draft the cover memo (or letter) for the audit boss's use. The same concern with clear and effective communication applies here, as this is the formal communication to the outside world.

As an auditor, your job is complete when the audit boss accepts your report. Sure, you will probably get involved in any correction activities after the report goes out. Or follow-up tasks may be done by others. The auditor's job is to report. The follow-up work is more of a consulting role. Follow-up also provides you with valuable feedback on how you did. You learn from your mistakes in logic or communication and become better. Be careful not to confuse the auditing and consulting.

Response Requested

If any problems were identified, they need to be tracked and resolved. Many years ago, we would issue an audit report containing findings. Each finding was tracked to completion. When all findings were closed, that audit was closed. Sometimes, it took several years to resolve a particularly tough finding. This gave the appearance that the audit program was not promptly identifying and resolving problems. Additionally, sometimes we lost track of the many issues. Auditors and bosses moved on and some of the information was lost.

Today, most audit programs use the corrective action system to track and resolve audit findings. This has several benefits:

- Tracking is generally better, so fewer things get lost.
- Auditors do a better job of finding and analyzing problems, knowing they are not responsible for fixing those same problems.
- Managers have a better picture of organizational issues. Problems from many sources (audit, maintenance, customers, regulators, and so on) go into the same pot (see Figure 5.7). It becomes easier to see the common control issues and thus resolve them.

The report package should have a Corrective Action Request (CAR) sheet for each finding sheet. See Figure 5.8 for an example form. You fill

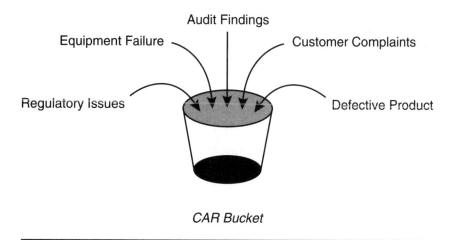

Figure 5.7 The corrective action pot.

CORRECTIVE ACTION REQUEST		CAR No.: 03-12
Issued to:	Andrew Sail	
Problem Statement:	Fixtures and equipment are not maintained in accordance with requirements.	
Short term (remedial) action already taken:		
Underlying (root) cause of the problem:		
Long tern (corrective) action planned:		
Milestones and responsibilities:		
Expected completion date:		
Manager signature and date:		
Follow-up and verification actions:		
CAR Closed:	By:	Date:

Figure 5.8 Illustration of finding to CAR.

out the top part. They fill out the middle part and send it back to the CAR boss, who will probably be someone other than the audit boss. We will discuss the corrective action system in greater detail in the next chapter.

When you transfer your findings to the corrective action sheets, just transfer the statement of the problem. Cause and effect, plus all the supporting bullets, stay on the finding sheets.

The audit boss should send an e-mail message to the auditee, summarizing the results and requesting a response to any corrective action sheets. Three things are attached to this e-mail message:

1. Your audit report (two pages)
2. Individual finding sheets (maximum of six)
3. Corrective action request (CAR) sheet for each finding

The message should request a written response, using the CAR sheets, to all findings within a stated time. We don't expect everything be fixed right away. Rather, we are asking for an action plan for correcting any problems. For supplier audits, 30 days from receipt of the report is not an unreasonable time period for putting together this kind of information. For internal system audits, two to four weeks is reasonable. For process audits, one to two weeks is more appropriate. Regardless of the times, make sure your audit boss specifies what is needed and when it is needed. Don't make the reader refer to some procedure hidden away in another area for guidance on the response.

DISTRIBUTION OF THE REPORT

Keep the distribution of your audit report small. If this information were to fall into the hands of your enemies or competitors, it could do damage to your firm. This is sensitive information and should be protected. If you send it to the boss of the auditee, you are saying, "I don't trust you, so I'm going to tell your boss." If you send copies to subordinates, you are saying, "I know better than you how to communicate to your group." Leave all of that further distribution to the auditee. Let the auditee decide if the results should be shared with one's boss or staff. This is not your call.

Within the United States, most regulatory agencies are not granted access to internal company audit reports. Likewise, internal audits are normally excluded from the legal discovery process. This is because most agencies recognize that society benefits from an active program of self-examination and cleansing. If we allow those reports to be seen by the regulators and lawyers, the incentive for self-examination becomes less. Why should we write ourselves up and give that information to the regulators, so they can fine us? Most government regulators can examine your audit schedules to see if you are looking in all the right areas. They want to see if the audit program is implemented. They will also want to know if problems uncovered are actually resolved. The regulators have instructions to stay away from the actual audit reports and field notes, though.

Audit report distribution was much easier before the days of the Internet, Intranets, wide area networks, virtual private networks, and the like. We would give our original report to the audit boss. The report with finding sheets, the CAR sheets, and the cover letter were copied as a package and sent out. The process today is much different. The days of paper-only distribution are forever gone. We know that very little information is private once it is released to the network. An e-mail message, once sent, cannot be unsent. It is difficult, if not impossible, to destroy virtual data with today's technologies. This is an area that is under development and study. We know that access to our reports should be restricted, but we do not know how to accomplish that objective. Attempts to date have included secure file servers, group file permission settings, and legal language at the bottom of all e-mail messages. None of these approaches has proven satisfactory yet. This is an area we are still exploring.

WRAP-UP

In this section we considered the audit report as your product. It is the only permanent feature of all the work that goes into the audit. It is important that the report be written as the work progresses, not in a rush at the end.

The most important part of the audit report is the summary. This overall analysis gives your audience a look at the health of the examined program from an outsider's perspective. Any problems identified through the audit must be presented such that stakeholders will take action on them. This requires that findings address the truly important business issues. They must be written in business language. You must show the pain, if you want any change to occur. You must present information in a fashion that will lead the reader to draw the same conclusions as the audit team.

The exit meeting is the first formal presentation of the audit results, although everyone should have a pretty good idea of the results if you practice the concept of no secrets and daily briefings. Following the exit meeting, the formal report is issued by the audit boss or purchasing agent.

ENDNOTES

1. Lawrence B. Sawyer, *The Practice of Modern Internal Auditing*, 2nd ed. (Altamonte Springs, FL: Institute of Internal Auditors, 1981): 3.
2. Charles E. Cuzzetto, "Auditing Management Reports," *Internal Auditor* 45 (December 1988): 36.
3. Until the publication of ISO 19011-2002, the term *finding* was not defined in audit standards. The General Accounting Office reports refer to *findings*, with the implication that they are significant problems and deficiencies. The *Generally Accepted Government Auditing Standards* require copies of audit reports to go to those responsible for action on audit findings, implying

something negative. The IIA's *Standards for the Professional Practice of Internal Auditing* state that action should be taken on reported audit findings. The term *audit conclusion* is used in both positive and negative lights. Other than an obscure standard on auditing nuclear materials safeguards (ANSI N15.38-1982), the term was not defined in the literature before publication of the second edition of this book.

4. The *seven basic tools* include flowcharts, control charts, cause-and-effect diagrams, histograms, check sheets, Pareto charts, and scatter diagrams. See the June through December 1990 issues of *ASQ Quality Progress* magazine for more details on these tools.

5. This phrase, *the vital few from the trivial many,* is often attributed to J. M. Juran. See J. M. Juran, *Quality Control Handbook,* 3rd ed. (New York: McGraw-Hill, 1974): 2–16, for a discussion on its origin and use.

6

FOLLOW-UP AND CLOSURE

CLOSURE PHASE

Auditing and corrective action are two closely related, but separate, quality management systems. (Recall that a system is a set of processes all working together to achieve a common objective.) If we assume that some of our audits will uncover problems, the output of auditing is the input of corrective action. This is especially true if you include CAR sheets in the audit package.

The *closure phase* of the audit starts after the formal report is issued. As discussed earlier, your job as an auditor is finished when the audit boss accepts your report and you have assembled all the records. This is theory. In reality, you will probably assist others in evaluating and perhaps resolving the identified problems. This means you need to understand remedial action, corrective action, and even preventive action.

REMEDIAL ACTION

Each of the bad facts listed under the audit finding requires *remedial action*. These are the immediate or short-term things done for each listed item. The auditee is expected to take remedial action on each of them.

Remedial action methods originate in inspection and test control systems. They were developed prior to WWII and used by the military during and after the war. Remedial action is always applied to nonconforming product (including services). You cannot perform remedial action on processes or systems.

If the results of the inspection do not conform to requirements, the item is declared nonconforming. After isolating the nonconforming item and branding it as defective, we must decide its disposition. These all begin with the letter R:

- **Rework.** This means to do the activity again. The physical item is not destroyed. It is sent through the processes again. You might sand away the paint and spray it again. You might recalibrate the instrument. You might rearrange the table setting. You might run the program again, this time with all the code modules loaded. You might require all staff to go through the training program again. You could enter missing information (or review notations) on a record.
- **Reject.** Throw the item away. It is of no use to anyone, except the scrap broker. Erase that offending code library file from the hard drive—it's just too buggy.
- **Repair.** Make it acceptable. It will work, but it is not exactly conforming. You didn't need the soup spoon anyway, so leave it off the table setting. Cut the bad part of the apple out. Grind away the unsatisfactory weld and apply more filler material.
- **Release.** It's good enough for the user, even though it doesn't meet all requirements. I accept the fact that all my people didn't attend the training session, but the activity is finished and life must go on. The release disposition is common in service applications, where it is difficult to do the task again. There are two subcategories of release, when working with tangible product.

    –*Re-grade.* Sell the (originally) nonconforming material at a lower price. The customer accepts the fact that all quality criteria have not been met, but knows a bargain when she sees it. Department stores do this quite often. So does the chemical industry. Food products that don't meet human consumption requirements might be satisfactory for farm animals.
    –*Recycle.* Take the nonconforming product and blend it into the processing stream. The good molecules and bad molecules get all mixed up and it becomes hard to tell them apart.

While the idea of remedial action started with tangible products, the same concept can be applied to all goods and services. You expect the auditee to take remedial action on all bad facts listed on your finding sheets. The actual disposition (one of the *R* items above) is up to the supervisor or manager of the audited area. You (or the audit boss) should not try to second-guess the decision. Even though you may not agree with it, you should keep quiet.

CORRECTIVE ACTION

The principle of *corrective action* is that conditions adverse to quality are identified and corrected. The cause of identified problems is determined. Steps are taken to preclude repetition. These steps include fixing the underlying cause and making sure the fix actually worked. True corrective action is probably the most difficult part of a quality management system to implement. The real underlying or root causes of problems are seldom easy to identify. But without an effective and objective corrective action program, the quality of all operations will suffer greatly.

The corrective action system has four linked processes (actions), which all work together to keep the problem from recurring:

1. Identify problems worthy of correcting.
2. Understand each problem's underlying (root) cause.
3. Fix the underlying cause conditions.
4. Make sure the changes work.

Identify Problems for Correcting

Corrective action takes a great deal of organizational energy. It is possibly one of the most difficult of all the quality systems explored over the last several decades. Organizations have a limited amount of this energy. It must be spent wisely. If you and your suppliers attempt to correct each and every identified problem and nonconformance, you will all waste that limited store of energy. You will burn out. So, you need to set a minimum threshold of pain before a problem is worthy of corrective action attention. As stressed earlier, the pain factors should be associated with business values. These are always cost, production, and risk. These are universal business drivers. They apply to service and manufacturing. They apply to government and industry. They apply to education, health-care delivery, and financial services. They apply everywhere.

Try not to confuse corrective action with remedial action. All identified nonconforming items need remedial action. Only problems that exceed the local pain threshold require corrective action.

Your pain threshold should be high enough to filter out the background noise, but low enough to achieve results before it is too late. If you wait until a fire destroys the warehouse, it is too late to work on the sprinkler system maintenance issues. There's nothing left to fix.

Through the audit, you have made this decision for the auditee. Because it is a finding, it is (by definition) worthy of corrective action. You even helped by entering each problem (from the finding sheets) into the corrective action tracking system. You attached a CAR sheet to the audit report package. You have declared, "This is a problem in need of fixing."

Determine the Underlying Cause

By listing the supporting bad facts under the finding, you have helped. Now the auditee must apply all the problem-solving tools to find the underlying (or root) cause. Teams, Pareto charts, nominal group techniques, and affinity diagrams are all ways to do this.[1] This is very difficult to do. It generally requires more than one person. It usually takes more than a day.

Fixing the Underlying Cause

Fixing the underlying cause requires change at the system level. New tools, new methods, increased or different skill levels, new capital equipment, and all manner of resources are but a few of the options. This takes time and money. Rarely can this level of change be done in less than a month.

Verify the Fix Really Worked

Even with the best minds of the company trying to solve a problem, sometimes we just don't get it right. The problem comes back. We didn't really understand it or failed someplace in implementing changes.

The last step in corrective action is to take a backward look to see if the problem is recurring. In some cases, constant change in markets, resources, or technologies will introduce enough variables to guarantee that the problem recurs. We need to analyze data to show that the problem remains fixed. We usually need a year's worth of data.

The audit program, along with normal management review and supervision, will address the first step of identifying problems needing solutions. But as was discussed in the previous section, you will make judgments that may result in different interpretations on the severity of the reported problem. This is why the identification of pain is so important in the way findings are presented in your audit report. If you show the disease, rather than just the symptom, the cause becomes obvious. It is the underlying reason for the pain. It is the cause of cause-and-effect analysis.

CORRECTIVE ACTION RESPONSE

After the audit report is issued, your audit job is mostly done. You enter the consulting phase. If any adverse conclusions (findings) are included, the auditee will send a response to the CAR sheets to the CAR boss. (Suppliers will send their responses to the buyer, who will send them on to the CAR boss.) This response is not a report that all problems have been fixed; rather, it sets forth the action to be taken. It is an action plan of things to come. For a supplier audit, 30 days from receipt of the audit report is the typical turnaround time for the response. For the internal system audit, the response should come in 15 to 30 days. For the small process audit, seven to 14 days is common. It is your duty, as the auditor, to make the response requirements and due dates very specific in the draft cover letter you prepare for the audit boss. You also need to cover the flow of information during the exit meeting with the auditee. It helps to hand out blank CAR sheets during the exit meeting as you explain the process.

Although you may discuss corrective action issues in the exit meeting, you probably will not get much of a substantive commitment in that period of high stress. Senior managers want to think it over before they make any real promises to change. This is normal.

This is your audit. You should continue to monitor the activities after it is issued. You have an obligation to see if wrongs are righted. You also need the feedback on your own performance. Check with the CAR boss or the purchasing agent as the response due date approaches. If a response does not come on time, you may be asked to have a face-to-face meeting with the tardy manager(s). If this doesn't work, someone higher up needs to call (or write if calls do not produce a response) to remind the audited organization of their need to positively commit to corrective action. These are all danger signs for your audit. You somehow did not convince. You made the report too complex. You didn't show cause and effect.

ADEQUACY OF THE RESPONSE

After receiving the response, the CAR boss may well ask you to evaluate its adequacy. You should try to include your audit team in this evaluation, if at all possible. You are looking for:

1. Identification of the underlying cause of the condition
2. Plans for fixing the underlying cause
3. Identification of specific managers responsible for the above
4. Due dates for accomplishing the corrections

Personal preference should not influence this evaluation. You must decide if the planned action makes sense and has a reasonable chance of success. At this point you should probably ease up on your expectations. You have expended most of your energy and persuasion devices. If things look like they will get better, accept the response.

In a very real way, the response given by the auditee is a direct measure of your performance as an auditor. If you write a good report, one that relates to business values and communicates to senior management, you will receive a good response. If your response is argumentative, you should look at yourself, rather than the auditee. (When you point your finger at someone, three of your fingers are pointing back to you.) What did you do to cause that miscommunication? How can you do better next time? The response is your report card. It is the best metric for the audit boss to use in evaluating the audit program.

There are, however, times when the response may be inadequate. Once this decision is made and your informal discussions are getting nowhere, you must ask for help from the audit boss, CAR boss, or contract administrator. It is here that the true strength of your audit program will show. If those folks truly believe in the value of auditing, they will back you up (and council you to produce better reports in the future). You should draft a letter or memo stating why the response is unacceptable and requesting a new response. The tone of this letter should be significantly more forceful than before.

If serious doubts about the effectiveness of corrective action plans continue and your management is unable to sway the auditee by discussion, request your audit boss to schedule a follow-up visit with the auditee to work out the problems. As a last resort for suppliers, your firm may wish to make effective corrective action on the findings a precondition for any additional business. Such drastic action means that the audit has failed in its original purpose.

RECORDS

Good records will convince others that you have an effective audit program. You examine records in your quest for the truth; others will do likewise. In addition, good records will help when preparing for the next regularly scheduled audit.

Audit records may be classified as either long-term or short-term records, depending upon their use and the length of time they are kept. Long-term records are kept for others.

While practices vary throughout the world, five to seven years is typical for keeping long-term records. After that, they probably won't mean very much. If you are in a regulated industry, such as pharmaceuticals or nuclear power, it could be longer. Check with your legal staff or contract administrators.

These are typical long-term records:

- Audit notification letter (or e-mail message) and audit plan
- Blank checklists
- Audit report and any forwarding letters or messages
- Completed CAR sheets

Short-term records are kept for your own use. They are not really used to prove anything. They help you prepare for the next audit in that area. They help when following up on identified problems. A good length of time to keep these records is one year or until the next audit of that area.

Typical short-term records are:

- Copies of auditor qualification records
- Completed checklists (work papers)
- Documents and records obtained from auditee
- Additional correspondence and messages

You may have noticed that completed checklists are not in the long-term category. Often, untrained auditors will examine your files, pull out your five-year-old notes, and ask why certain decisions were made. By periodically purging these limited-use records, you have fewer sources of unnecessary discomfort.

A good way to keep paper records is to assemble everything from a particular audit into two folders: long-term and short-term. Set aside one file cabinet or file drawer for these audit records. After the audit boss accepts the report, assemble all associated records and place them in the proper folder. Periodically, purge the folders to make room for new ones.

Things have changed considerably as we transition to virtual records. Networking and computers allow us to keep nearly everything, almost forever. Destruction of electronic records is quite difficult to completely accomplish. On the other hand, they become easy to lose at the press of a button. Virtual records also have the potential to be altered or manipulated, either by accident or malicious intent. As with everything else, though, the concepts remain the same. Keep the short-term records handy and easy to access. Protect the long-term records from premature loss, either accidental or deliberate.

A RECAP

In this chapter we considered the activities that take place after your report package goes out. After the audit boss accepts your report, you tidy up the records associated with your recent assignment. Others may do most of the follow up on identified problems. The response is evaluated. This is your report card. If you do a good audit, you get a good response. The auditee and others will perform corrective action on your identified problems. This includes analyzing the problem for underlying cause, fixing the underlying cause, and making sure the fix really worked. All of this is very difficult and takes considerable resources.

ENDNOTE

1. Nancy R. Tague, *The Quality Toolbox* (Milwaukee: ASQC Quality Press, 1995).

7

SUMMARY

You have seen how the basic monitoring methods originally developed by accountants can be used to improve any type of activity, large or small, internal or external. The keys to success are no different here than in any other business venture.

- Thorough preparation
- Rigorous performance
- Meaningful reporting
- Effective follow-up

Whether you perform audits of the processes used to make various items, the performance of other departments, or the actions of your suppliers, you use the same basic auditing skills. These skills come from formal training coupled with real-life practice. Skilled auditors are one of your organization's greatest assets. They know the enterprise and its processes, people, and procedures. They understand internal and external customer relationships. And they possess the ability to communicate to others.

Ideally, auditors should possess a balance of emotional, mechanical, and intellectual skills. They must be able to conduct interviews, control a hostile group, convince a skeptical audience, and understand different perspectives. They must also be skilled in the mechanics of sampling, tracing, analysis, and other forms of data processing. Finally, they must be able to organize a campaign and communicate to their fellow humans. These are not easy skills to obtain. They can only be developed through study, practice, and feedback.

The audit boss, who is in charge of the audit program, must demand excellence and provide feedback. If one allows poor reports to be published, then eventually all reports will achieve that level of mediocrity. If the audit program does not contribute to the betterment of the firm or agency, it should not be allowed to survive. Thus, it is important to always remember that the goal of auditing is to improve the performance of the audited activity.

Auditing can be reduced down to four basic rules:

1. Audits provide information to others.
2. Auditors are qualified to perform their tasks.
3. Audits measure to agreed criteria.
4. Conclusions are based on fact.

Periodically, you should examine your own audit program to see if these rules are still being followed.

This text has presented you with basic concepts and theories of the quality audit process. It has also identified some practical ways to implement the theory. As the application of quality auditing becomes more established, certain methods will grow and others will die. This is to be expected. Auditing, like all the soft sciences, is an evolutionary process. Regardless of the changes, though, the purpose of the audit will always be to provide interested parties with meaningful information upon which to base decisions. Through proper application, these decisions will cause performance to improve (see Figure 7.1).

Figure 7.1 Improved performance!

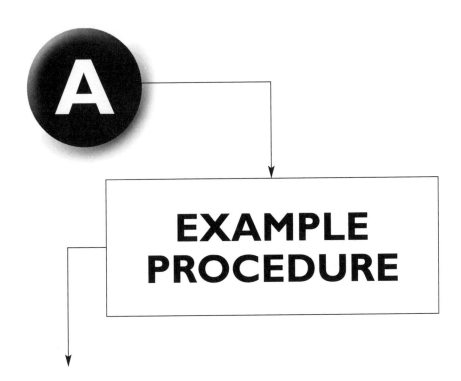

PURPOSE AND SCOPE

This procedure covers the planning and performance of internal system audits. Internal process audits are under the control of each functional department and are controlled through the use of functional department procedures. This procedure does not address auditing of external suppliers, or the manner in which we respond to audits performed on our activities by our customers or regulators.

DEFINITIONS

- **Audit Team Leader:** A person who is qualified and authorized to manage and direct an audit. Also known as the Lead Auditor.
- **Audit Team Member:** A person who is qualified to assist a Team Leader in performing a portion of an audit assignment. Also known as an Auditor.
- **Audit Finding:** An audit conclusion that identifies a condition having a significant adverse effect on the quality of the activity under review.
- **Positive Practice:** An audit conclusion which identifies a condition of exceptional merit.

- **Document:** A written description of an activity to be accomplished.
- **Record:** A written description of an activity that has been accomplished.

PERSONNEL QUALIFICATION

All auditors shall perform their duties in an unbiased and objective manner. Auditors shall not be assigned to audit an area in which they have had a material design or development role. This restriction shall be in effect for a period of one year from such participation.

Audit Team Leaders shall demonstrate their competence to the AUDITS MANAGER prior to leading an audit. The AUDITS MANAGER is responsible for qualifying all Audit Team Leaders based upon: (1) demonstrated knowledge of the technical processes to be audited, (2) oral and written communication abilities, and (3) ability to lead a team. Unless they possess a valid CQA certificate issued by ASQ, Audit Team Leaders shall participate in at least two audits prior to being qualified as a team leader.

Audit Team Members shall be qualified to the requirements specified by the audit's TEAM LEADER. This qualification is only valid for the period of the specific audit being conducted.

SCHEDULING

Internal system audits shall be performed in a cost-effective manner consistent with the needs of internal and external customers and available resources. Annual audit planning shall be conducted in the first quarter after the new fiscal year. By the end of the first quarter of each year, the AUDITS MANAGER shall prepare an Annual Audit Planning Schedule based upon the following criteria:

- **Cost.** High-dollar activities shall be audited before low-dollar areas. Factors to consider should be contract amount, personnel assigned, importance to some national effort, and potential for scrap or waste.
- **Risk.** High-risk activities shall receive priority in audit planning. Factors to consider should be safety to employees, potential for environmental damage, and possible loss of capital equipment.
- **Management Requests.** Those areas receiving the greatest management attention should be audited before areas in need of little attention. The needs of the customer shall also be considered.

- **Department or Section.** At least one audit shall be scheduled each year to examine the implementation of the company QA program within each Department or Section. This is considered to be above and beyond the annual appraisal of QA program effectiveness required by company policy.
- **Administrative Activity.** Because the following activities affect all projects and programs within the company, they shall be scheduled individually. Other activities may be added as required.

–Procurements
–Records management
–Document control
–General employee training

The Annual Audit Planning Schedule shall identify audited activities and the month in which they are scheduled for audit. No further definition (specific dates, auditors, requirements, and so on) is required or desired. The Annual Audit Planning Schedule shall be approved by the PLANT MANAGER and distributed to all departments and sections within the company by the QUALITY ASSURANCE DIRECTOR. The Annual Audit Planning Schedule may be modified but once before a new schedule must be prepared and distributed.

Quarterly Audit Planning Schedules shall be developed by the AUDITS MANAGER, based upon the annual audit planning schedule. These quarterly schedules shall contain the following information:

- Audited activity (from annual schedule)
- Start date
- Audit team leader

Quarterly schedules shall be distributed by the AUDITS MANAGER to all affected project or program managers, and others as deemed necessary, prior to the start of each quarter. These schedules may be modified to suit circumstances, as long as all planned audits are performed within the affected quarter. Should any audits appearing on the annual plan be deferred during the affected quarter, the reason for such deferral shall be reported to the QUALITY ASSURANCE DIRECTOR.

AUDIT PLANNING

Prior to the performance of an audit, an *Audit Plan* shall be prepared and appropriate parties shall be notified. *Audit Plans* shall be prepared by the AUDIT TEAM and contain the following information:

- Audit title and number
- Auditee
- Purpose
- Scope
- Requirements
- Organizations affected
- Any interfaces
- Team members
- Overall schedule
- Review and approval

Another auditor shall review the *Audit Plan*. The AUDIT TEAM LEADER shall present the audit plan to the AUDITS MANAGER for approval. Additionally, the team leader shall draft a notification memo from the AUDITS MANAGER to the affected activity manager(s). The notification memo should summarize the information contained in the *Audit Plan* and include the plan as an attachment. Every effort should be made to notify the auditee, by e-mail, at least 30 days in advance of an impending audit. Audit team members should also receive a copy of the notification memo and plan.

Written checklist questions shall be developed for each audit prior to the commencement of the opening meeting. These checklist questions shall act as a guide to the audit team in performing their investigation in order to assure that all important elements of the control system are examined. As such, they may be written in any format found to be useful to the individual auditor(s). They shall, however, include examination questions covering each control element specified in the audit base (requirement documents). Checklists shall be developed individually for each audit, but may include questions from previous audits and standard lists. In order to provide for added assurance that checklist questions are adequate for the audited area, a qualified audit team leader, other than the originator, shall review each checklist. This review shall be indicated by the word "reviewed" and a signature and date somewhere on the front page of each checklist. Checklists may be informally provided to the auditee prior to the fieldwork.

PERFORMANCE

Fieldwork shall commence with a brief opening meeting between the audit team and the management of the area to be audited. Blank copies of the checklists to be used for the audit shall be distributed at the opening meeting. (This is in addition to any informal copies provided earlier.)

The audit shall be performed such that elements selected for examination are evaluated for conformance and effectiveness against specified requirements. Objective evidence shall be examined to the degree necessary to determine if the control elements are being effectively implemented. The results of this examination (positive and negative facts) should be recorded on the checklist pages or on supplemental notes. Every effort should be made to keep the auditee apprised of the progress of the audit and concerns of the audit team. For audits lasting longer than a day, the auditee shall be briefed at the end of each day.

AUDIT REPORT

Each audit shall conclude with a brief closing (exit) meeting between the audit team and the management of the area audited. Copies of the draft audit conclusions (or summary), along with any draft *Findings* or *Positive Practices* should be provided to those in attendance.

Within one week of the closing meeting, the Audit Report shall be prepared in the form of a memo from the AUDIT TEAM LEADER to the AUDITS MANAGER. The Audit Report shall contain the following information:

- Audit title, number, and other identifying information
- Background information, such as audit purpose, scope, dates, audit team members, and procedures used, plus a brief description of the activities audited and any affected customers (one paragraph)
- Summary and overall conclusions of the effectiveness of the quality program as implemented by the audited organization(s)
- An executive summary of any Findings or Positive Practices and how they affect products or deliverables
- Specific Finding Sheets or Positive Practice Sheets as attachments

Audit Findings shall be presented as a generic statement of the nonconforming condition and its affect on business operations. This is followed by discussion (or explanation) points. The first point should be a description of the specific requirement(s) for the control item under question. Then list two or more examples of specific objective evidence, found during the course of the audit, supporting the conclusion that a significant adverse condition exists. Positive Practices shall be presented in a fashion similar to Audit Findings, except that examples cited are good, rather than bad, practices.

After the AUDITS MANAGER has accepted the Audit Report (with any attachments), it shall be provided by e-mail to the affected manager(s) from the AUDITS MANAGER. The forwarding message shall request corrective action as applicable. If the report includes any Audit Findings, Corrective Action Request (CAR) sheets shall be included for use by the addressee. Generally, a response to each CAR should be requested such that a reply is received within 30 days of the audit report date. The AUDITS MANAGER should send a copy of the report and CAR sheets to the audit team and keep a printed copy for the audit files.

FOLLOW-UP

The CORRECTIVE ACTION COORDINATOR shall evaluate responses for effective corrective action. The audit team shall assist in this evaluation as requested. Specifically, replies to CAR sheets shall verify that:

- Remedial action is listed for the individual facts.
- The cause of the problem is stated.
- Actions are appropriate to correct the cause of the problem.
- Specific responsibilities and dates for corrective action have been identified.

Once the above has been obtained and any follow-up verification has been completed, the CORRECTIVE ACTION COORDINATOR shall complete the bottom of the CAR sheets to indicate closure.

The AUDITS MANAGER shall periodically review the status of audit-generated CAR sheets. The AUDITS MANAGER shall prepare a quarterly report to the DIRECTOR OF QUALITY ASSURANCE on the following four items:

1. Audits scheduled and completed during the quarter
2. Significant new issues that have arisen
3. Progress made on resolving old issues
4. Areas in need of senior management attention

This information shall be provided in time for the quarterly management review meetings.

RECORDS

The following items are considered to be long-term audit records. They are primarily for use by outsiders (customers and regulators). Paper copies, in addition to electronic files, shall be maintained by the AUDITS MANAGER for five years:

- Audit Notification Message and Audit Plan
- Blank Audit Checklists

- Audit Report and forwarding message
- Completed Corrective Action Request (CAR) sheets

The following items are considered to be working audit records. They are primarily for use in resolving problems in an area just audited and for preparing for another audit in the same area later on. The AUDITS MANAGER shall maintain these working records for a period of one year, or until the next audit in the area, after which time they may be discarded:

- Audit team qualification records
- Audit field notes and other working papers
- Related miscellaneous correspondence
- Annual Audit Schedules and any revisions
- Quarterly Audit Schedules
- Superseded Auditing Procedures (marked archive)

FORMS

Examples of forms used in the administration of the audit program are attached. These may be modified at the discretion of the AUDITS MANAGER.

GLOSSARY OF TERMS

Appraisal—A form of the system audit, normally conducted to examine the total management system effectiveness and implementation. An appraisal is often conducted by a contracted third party and reported to the very highest levels of management.

Assessment—An evaluation of management system conformity to industry, national, or international standards. The term comes from *conformity assessment,* which was originally developed for international trade assurances of delivered product quality.

Audit—An independent, structured, and reported examination and analysis to see that something is as it should be. An audit may examine any portion of the management control spectrum, including financial, environmental, and quality aspects of business and government.

Audit (ISO 19011-2002)—A systematic, independent, and documented process for obtaining audit evidence and evaluating it objectively to determine the extent to which audit criteria are fulfilled.

Audit client (ISO 19011-2002)—The organization or person requesting an audit.

Audit criteria (ISO 19011-2002)—The set of policies, procedures, or requirements.

Audit evidence—See *objective evidence.*

Audit program—The collection of methods used to plan, perform, report, and manage audits.

Audit program (ISO 19011-2002)—A set of one or more audits planned for a specific time frame and directed toward a specific purpose.

Audit program manager—The person responsible for managing the audit program. Sometimes called the *client*. This person is accountable to senior management for success of the audit program. Also known as the *Audit Boss.*

Audit standard—A written description of essential audit characteristics, reflecting current thought and practice. The three most common standards come from ISO (quality management system audits), IIA (internal corporate audits), and GAO (government audits).

Audit team—One or more qualified auditors.

Audit team (ISO 19011-2002)—One or more auditors conducting an audit, supported if needed by technical experts.

Audit team leader— A person who is qualified and authorized to manage and direct an audit. Also known as a *Lead Auditor.*

Audit team member—See *auditor* below.

Auditee—The organization being audited. The auditee may be an internal group within the firm or agency or it may be a contractor organization.

Auditor—A person who is qualified to assist an Audit Team Leader in performing a portion of an audit assignment. Also known as an *Audit Team Member.*

Certification (of auditors and team leaders)—The act of determining, verifying, and attesting to the qualifications of a person to perform effective audits in accordance with applicable requirements. Certification may be internal (by the person's employer) or external (by a professional society such as the American Society for Quality or the Institute of Internal Auditors).

Characteristic—Any distinct property of an item or activity that can be described and measured. The ANSI/ISO/ASQ Q9000-2000 standard lists several classes of characteristics, such as physical, sensory, behavioral, temporal, ergonomic, and functional.

Compliance—A product or activity that meets required characteristics and was performed or produced in accordance with required process and system requirements. Compliance may be thought of as the output of one or more processes and the controls under which those processes occurred.

Confirmation—The agreement of data obtained from two or more different sources.

Conformity—Meets required characteristics. Usually determined through inspection.

Conformity (ANSI/ISO/ASQ Q9000-2000)—Fulfillment of a requirement.

Corrective action—Action taken to eliminate the causes of an existing undesirable condition, in order to minimize or prevent its recurrence.

Corrective action (ANSI/ISO/ASQ Q9000-2000)—Action to eliminate the cause of a detected nonconformity or other undesirable situation.

Corroboration—Confirmation of information obtained by an interview.

Desk audit—Slang term for the evaluation of lower-tier documents to higher-tier requirements before fieldwork starts. It should not be confused with a questionnaire sent to gather information.

Document—A written description of an activity to be accomplished. (See also *Record.*)

Document (ANSI/ISO/ASQ Q9000-2000)—Information and its supporting medium.

Evaluation—The act of examining a product, process, or system to requirements and forming conclusions as a result.

Examination—A measurement of goods, services, or knowledge to determine conformance to some requirement. Examination provides the input for evaluation.

External audit—An audit performed on a supplier by a customer or agent.

Extrinsic audit—An audit performed on you by your customer.

Finding—An audit conclusion that identifies a condition having a significant adverse effect on the quality of the activity under review. A finding is a problem or cause-and-effect statement and is normally accompanied by several specific examples of the observed condition.

Finding (ISO 19011-2002)—Results of the evaluation of the collected audit evidence against audit criteria.

Follow-up—Verifying that some corrective action has been accomplished as promised.

Guidelines—Methods that are considered good practice but that are not mandatory. Generally, the term *should* means a guideline and the term *shall* means a requirement.

Independent—Not directly responsible for the quality, cost, and/or production of goods and services being examined.

Inspection (ANSI/ISO/ASQ Q9000-2000)—Conformity evaluation and judgment accompanied as appropriate by measuring, testing, or gauging.

Lead auditor—A person who is qualified and authorized to manage and direct an audit. Also known as an *audit team leader.*

Nonconformity (ANSI/ISO/ASQ Q9000-2000)—The nonfulfillment of a requirement.

Objective evidence (ANSI/ISO/ASQ Q9000-2000)—Data supporting the existence or verity of something. Also *audit evidence* (ISO 19011-2002)—Records, statements of fact, or other information which are relevant to the audit criteria and verifiable.

Process audit—The evaluation of a process operation against all (input, output, and processing) requirements. The process audit measures conformance to input and output characteristics and the effectiveness of process controls. It is sometimes called a *surveillance.*

Product audit—A re-inspection and re-test of product that has already been accepted or a review of records for that product. It is not a true audit, but rather an inspection. It is sometimes called a [shipping] *dock audit.*

Quality assurance (ANSI/ISO/ASQ Q9000-2000)—That part of quality management focusing on providing confidence that quality requirements will be fulfilled.

Quality audit—An *audit* that examines quality aspects of a product, process, or system.

Record—A written description of an activity that has been accomplished. (See also *document.*)

Record (ANSI/ISO/ASQ Q9000-2000)—A document stating results achieved of providing evidence of activities performed.

Specification (ANSI/ISO/ASQ Q9000-2000)—A document stating requirements.

Standard—A description of essential characteristics of an item or activity that has been agreed to by affected parties. Standards may be product specific (such as Grade A beef), process specific (such as TCP/IP for Internet data exchange), or system specific (such as ANSI/ISO/ASQ Q9001-2000 for quality management).

Surveillance—See *process audit.*

Survey—An activity conducted prior to a contract award and used to evaluate the quality or technical capabilities of a prospective supplier or contractor.

System audit—A structured activity performed to verify that one or more portions of a management program are appropriate and are effectively implemented in accordance with agreed-to standards of performance.

Index

A

accountability, audit manager and, 23–24
American Society for Quality (ASQ), 39
appraisal, defined, 127
ASQC C1, 2
assessment, defined, 127
audit applications, performance, 9
audit boss, 27, 118
audit categories, table, 17
audit checklist(s), 64–65
  blank, 124
  figure, 58
audit client, defined, 127
audit criteria, defined, 127
audit document, defined, 120
audit evidence, defined, 128
audit finding(s), 123
  defined, 119
audit follow-up, 124
  audits manager and, 124
  and closure, 109–116
    corrective action, 111–113
    records, 114–115
    remedial action, 109–111
    summary, 116
audit interview techniques, 73–77
audit notification message, 124
audit performance, 67–81
  daily briefings and, 80
  fact-gathering and, 70
  interviews and, 72–77
  opening meeting, 67–68
  perceptions and, 78
  team meetings and, 79
  tracing and, 71–72
audit plan, 48–49
  audit preparation, 64

audit plan *(continued)*
    formal notification, 51
    for process audit, figure, 50
    for system audit, figure, 49
audit planning, 121–122
    administrative activity, 121
    audits manager and, 121–122
    cost, 120
    department/section, 121
    fieldwork and, 122
    management requests, 120
    performance and, 122–123
    risk, 120
    schedule, 120–121
        table, 69
audit preparation, 29–65
    audit plan and, 48–49, 64
    audit team and, 33–35
    auditor's duties in, 35
    authority, 40–42
    documentation evaluation, 52
    forms of data, 54–55
    initial informal contact, 45
    initial informal contact, 45–46
    patterns, 56
    phases, 29–30
    process approach, 61
    purpose, 30–31
    requirements, 41–42
    scope, 32–33
    sense information, 55
    summary, 64
    understanding the process,
        46–47
    work papers, 54–57
audit program
    defined, 128
    independent, 34
    manager, 23–27, 31, 128
        accountability, 23–24
        audit schedule, 24
        resources for, 24–25

        problem-solving, 111–112
        resources for, 23–24
audit quality programs, origins,
    2–3
audit record(s)
    defined, 120
    audits manager and, 124
    long-term, 115
    paper, 115
    short-term, 115–116
    working, 125
audit relationships, 27
audit report, 123–124
    forwarding message and,
        125
    corrective action response,
        113–114
audit schedule(s), 24
    internal/external, 25–26
audit standard, defined, 128
audit(s)
    basis, 4, 41
    client, defined, 27
    compliance, 6–7, 17
        performance and, table, 9
        shortcomings, 8–9
    conclusions of, 5
    controls and, 16
    defined, 4, 18, 127
    evidence, 4
    extrinsic, 6
    financial, 6
    findings of, 5
    first party, 5
    high-risk, 7
    horizontal, 16
    internal, 5, 17
        defined, 18
    management, 9
    observation, 4
    one-person, problem, 34
    performance, 9–11, 17

phases of, 29
philosophy, 20–21
practices and processes,
    37–38
problem-solving, 111–113
process, 12–15, 17
    overview, 15
product, 11–12
product, 17
purpose, 30–31
registration, 7
regulatory, 7
reporting, 83–106
    cause and effect, 87
    characteristics, 83–84
    conclusions, 94
    distribution, 101–106
    exit meeting, 94
    finding sheets, prepar-
        ing, 86
    findings, 86
    formal report, 97
    inferences and, 84–85
    information presenta-
        tion, 92
    judgment and, 90
    judgments and, 85
    pain and pleasure, 85
    recommendations, 91
    summary, 106
    trust and, 84
scope of, 32–33
second party, 6
self, 5
sense information, 55
system, 15–17, 33
    defined, 131
tax, 6
team, 33–34
    competence, 37–39
        defined, 128
    independence, 34

leader, 27, 123
    defined, 119, 128
    member(s), 34–35
    defined, 119
    objectivity, 36
    practices and processes,
        37–38
    qualification, 36–39
    size/composition, 35–36
third party, 6, 17
types of, table, 17
value-added, 9
vertical, 17
auditee, defined, 128
auditing model, figure, 5
auditing procedures, summary,
    117–118
auditing standards
    government, 2
    origins, 2
auditing
    definitions, 119–120
    example procedure, 119–125
    general model of, 4–5
    history of, 1–3
    military and, 2
    nuclear and, 2
    process approach to, 61–62
    rules for, 19, 118
    summary, 117–118
auditor
    authority, 40
    defined, 128
    document and, 41
    duties, 35
    emotional skills, 37–38
    external requirements of, 42
    independence, 34
    lead, defined, 119
    professional qualification,
        39–40
    qualification(s), 36–40

auditor *(continued)*
    reports, positive vs. negative,
      20
    requirements, 41–42
    skills, figure, 38
    team leader, duties, 35
    technical competence of, 37
    types of, 4–6
audit(s) manager, 123–124
    duties, 120
    and audits records, 124
    audit planning and, 121–122
    records and, 125
authority, auditor, 40
authority, quality management
    system and, 40–41

B

basis of audit, 4, 41
bias, audit reporting, 91
blank audit checklists, 124
briefings, audit performance
    and, 80–81
British auditing, 3
BS7229 (1989), 3

C

call center, 71
Canadian auditing standard
    (CAN-Q395), 3
    quality standard, 3
    client defined, 27
CAR; *see* corrective action
    request
cause and effect findings, 87–88
    sheet, figure, 90
certificate of compliance, 7
certificate of conformance, 7
certificate of qualification, audi-
    tor, 39
certification, defined, 128

certification and registration, 6
Certified Quality Auditor, certifi-
    cation, 39–40
characteristic, defined, 128
checklist(s), 62–63
    assignments, 63
    daily briefings and, 80–81
    history and, 63–64
    use of, 57–58
client, audit, defined, 27
collecting evidence, tracing,
    71–72
collection plan, 59–61
    figure, 60
common goal, process to
    achieve, 12–13
compliance
    audit, 6–9, 17
    or conformance, 7–8
    defined, 129
    malicious, 91
    shortcomings, 8–9
conclusions of audit, 5
confirmation, defined, 129
conformance or compliance,
    7–8
conformity
    assessment program, 3, 7
    assessment qualification, 40
    defined, 129
controls, audit and 16
corporate auditors, origin, 2
corrective action
    audit, 111–113
    coordinator, 124
    defined, 129
    problems, 111
    request (CAR), 103–104
    response, 113–114
corroboration, defined, 129
cost, audit planning and, 120

customers of auditor, figure, 31
Cuzzetto, Charles, 106

D

daily briefings, 80–81
desk audit, defined, 129
distribution of formal report,
106–106
document(s)
    audit, defined, 120
    auditor, 41
    control, system, figure, 13
    defined, 13, 129
    evaluation, 52–53
        figure, 52
    external, 42–43
    levels, figure, 42
    transition, 43
documentation, auditing,
    43–44
duties of auditor, 35

E

emotional skills, auditor, 37–38
environmental auditors, 3–4
evaluation, defined, 129
evidence, collecting/tracing,
    71–72
evidence of audit, 4
examination, defined, 129
example procedure, auditing,
    119–125
exit meeting
    attendance, 95
    audit reporting, 94–97
    conducting, 95–97
    draft conclusions, 96
external audit, 6
    defined, 129
    schedule, table, 26
external documents, 42–43

external requirements, auditor, 42
extrinsic audit, 6, 129

F

fact-gathering, audit perform-
    ance and, 70; *see also* findings.
factory processes, figure, 14
fieldwork, audit planning and,
    122
fieldwork, same as audit per-
    formance, 67–81
figures
    audit checklists, 58
    audit plan for process audit,
        50
    audit plan for system audit,
        49
    audit planning schedule, 69
    auditing model, 5
    auditor skills, 38
    collection plan, 60
    corrective action request,
        103, 104
    document evaluation, 52
    document levels, 42
    factory processes, 14
    finding sheet, 89, 90
    formal audit report, 101
    PDCA (plan, do, check, act),
        19
    perceptions, example of, 78
    problem statement, finding
        sheet, 90
    process approach, 62
    process model for designer
        cells, 62
    process system model, 13
    product, process and system
        relationships, 44
    quality management system
        process, 13

figures *(continued)*
    tracing, 71
    universal process forces, 14
financial audit, 6
finding(s)
    audit, 5, 123
    audit reporting and, 86–91
    cause and effect, 87–88
    defined, 129–130
    sheet, 88–90
        with cause and effect,
            figure, 89
    statements, development, 86
first-party audits, 5
flowchart
    process approach, 61–62
    use of, 37, 57
follow-up and closure, audit,
    109–116; *see also* audit
    follow-up and closure
follow-up, defined, 130
formal notification, audit
    plan, 51
formal report, 97–107
    attachments, 100
    audit report, figure, 101
    corrective action request,
        103–104
    distribution, 101, 105–106
    findings, 100
    introduction, 98–99
    positive practices, 100
    release of, 102
    response request, 103
    size, 101
    summary, 98–99, 106

G

goals, systems/process to
    achieve, 12–13
Government Auditing Standards
    (1981), 2

guidelines, defined, 130

H

high-risk audit, 7
history of auditing, 1–2
history, checklists and, 63–64
horizontal audit, 16
hospital/hotels, product audit
    and, 11

I

IEEE Std. 1028, 3
improvement, management
    system and, 18
independence, of auditor, 34
independent, defined, 130
inferences, audit reporting, 84–85
information presentation, audit
    reporting, 92
initial informal contact, 45–46
initial meeting, for audit, 67–68
inspection, defined, 130
inspection, product audit and,
    11–12
Institute of Electrical and
    Electronic Engineers
    Standard 1028, 3
Institute of Internal Auditors
    (IIA), 2
internal audit, 5, 17
    defined, 18
    schedule, table, 25
internal system audit, corrective
    action response and, 113–114
interviews, audit, 72–77
    techniques of, 73–77
Ishikawa, Kaoru, 13, 22
ISO 9000 (2000), 12, 15
ISO 9001 (1987), 7
    origin, 3
ISO 10011-1 (1990), 3, 27, 56
ISO 14001, 3

ISO 19011, 4, 18, 27, 56, 127
  auditor independence and, 34

J

judgment, audit reporting and, 85
Juran, J. M., 107

L

lead auditor, defined, 119, 130
Leonard, William, 9, 22
long-term audit records, 115

M

machinery, defined, 14
Malcolm Baldrige National Qualilty Award, 11
malicious compliance, audit reporting, 91
management
  audit, 9
  principles, 18–19
  requests, audit planning, 120
  standard, 2
  system, 18
manpower (womanpower), defined, 14
material, defined, 14
measurement, defined, 14
measurement, management system and, 18
meeting, exit, 94–97; *see also* exit meeting
meeting, opening for audit, 67–68
meetings, team, audit performance and, 79
methods, defined, 13
military, auditing and, 2
Mills, Charles, 9

MIL-Q-9858, 2
model, auditing, 4–5

N

nonconformity, defined, 130
nuclear auditing, 2

O

objective evidence,
  defined, 130
  work papers, 56
objectivity, auditor, 36–37
observation of audit, 4
observations, auditing phase, 56
observations, U.S. General Accounting Office, 56
opening meeting, audit performance and, 67–68
operational audits, origin, 2
ownership of quality, 92

P

pain/pleasure of audit reporting, 85–86
paper records, audit, 115
patterns, work papers, 56
PDCA (plan, do, check, act), 8, 11, 41, 44
  figure, 19
perceptions,
  audit performance and, 78–79
  example, figure, 78
performance
  audit applications, 10
  audit(s), 9–11, 17; *see also* audit performance
  management system and, 18
personnel qualification, 120
planning schedule, audit, 69, 120–121

planning, management system and, 18
positive practice
  defined, 119
  statements, development, 86
practices and processes, auditing, 37–38
preparation of audit, 29–65
presention of information, audit reporting, 92
principles of management, 18–19
problem-solving, determine/fix cause(s), 112
problem statement, finding sheet, figure, 90
procedures, auditing, summary, 117–118
process, defined, 12
process approach to auditing, 61–62
process audit, 12–15, 17
  defined, 130
  exit meeting
    attendance, 95
    audit reporting, 94–97
    conducting, 95–97
    draft conclusions, 96
  overview, 15
  plan for, figure, 50
process forces, universal, 13–14
process model for designer cells, figure, 62
process system, model, figure, 13
process, product, and system relationships, 44–45
product audit, 11–12, 17
  inspection and, 11
product, process, and system relationships, 44

professional qualification, auditor, 39–40
purpose of audit, 30–31

Q
Q10011 (1994), 3
qualifications
  of auditor, 36–40
  of personnel, 120
quality, ownership, 92
quality assurance
  defined, 130
  director, 121, 124
quality auditing, 3
quality audits, rules for, 32, 40, 45, 54
quality management
  principle, 12
  standard, 2
  system(s)
    authority and, 40–41
    origins, 3
    processes, figure, 13
quality record, defined, 130

R
recommendations, audit reporting, 91–93
record, audit, defined, 120, 130–131
records, audit follow-up and closure, 114–115
registration and certification, 6
registration audit, 7
regulatory audit, 7
releasing the report, 102
report
  audit, 123–124
  characteristics, audit, 83–84
  formal, 97–107

attachments, 100
audit report, figure, 101
corrective action request,
103–104
distribution, 101, 105–106
findings, 100
introduction, 98–99
positive practices, 100
release of, 102
response request, 103
size, 101
summary, 98–99, 106
release of 102
size of, 101
reporting, audit, 83–106; *see also*
audit reporting
requirements of auditor, 41–42
response request, formal report,
103
risk, audit planning and, 120
rules for auditing, 19
rules for quality audits, 32, 40,
45, 54

S

Sawyer, Lawrence, 9, 21, 106
Sayle, Allan, 9, 22
scheduling criteria, 120–121
second-party audits, 6
self audit, 5
short-term audit records, 115–116
single audit, problems, 34
small process audit, corrective
action response and, 113–114
Software Reviews and Audits (IEEE
Std. 1028), 3
specification, defined, 131
Standard 1028 (IEEE), 3
standard, defined, 131
summary, auditing, 117–118
surveillance, defined, 131

survey, defined, 131
system, process, and product
relationships, 44–45
system audit, 15–17, 33, 131
plan for, figure, 49
table(s)
audit planning schedule,
69
audits, types of, 17
compliance and performance
audit, 10
external audit schedule, 26
internal audit schedule, 25

T

Tague, Nancy, 116
tax audit, 6
team leader, audit, 119–120, 123
duties, 35
team meetings, audit performance and, 79
team size/composition, 35–36
team, audit, 33–34
technical competence, auditor,
37
third-party audit(s), 6, 17
Three Mile Island incident, 8
tracing,
collecting evidence, 71–72
figure, 71
transition documents, 43

U

U.S. Federal Aviation
Administration, 11
U.S. General Accounting Office
auditing standards, 2
observations, 56
universal process forces, 13–14
figure, 14

V

value-added audit, 9
vertical audit, 17

W

work papers, 54–61
    checklists, 62–63
    collection plan, 59–61
    documents and records,
        55–56
    forms of data, 54–55

    objective evidence, 56
    patterns, 56
    physical properties, 55
    types of, 57

Y

"Yellow Book," 2

Z

Z-1.15 (1979), quality standard, 3